The Backwards Way

An Introduction to the
Theory and Methods
of the Order of the Voltec

Iremoch VI°
&
Wendigo V°

Voltec Publishing

© 2008 Voltec Publishing

http://www.redpath.imagitronix.co.za/voltec/

Copyright 2008 Voltec Publishing
redsect73@yahoo.com

ISBN: 978-0-6152-1214-2

Table of Contents

Preface...4

Introduction...7

What is "Voltec"?...18

History and Evolution of the
Order of the Voltec...20

Carlos Castaneda and the Core Concepts...25

The Assemblage Point...28

The Tree of Night...35

Theory and Practice within the
Order of the Voltec...45

Internal Structure and the Degree System
of the Order of the Voltec...79

Affiliation and Admissions Policies...101

Conclusion?...104

Bibliography...105

The Nine "Not-Doings" of the Voltec...107

Preface

The occult community has seen its ups and downs throughout history. In the past decade or so, an extreme decline in relevant Work and in valuable publications has forced true Seekers to sift through tons of worthless garbage in order to find a gram of usable information. The internet and "print on demand" publishing is truly a two-edged sword. They are powerful tools that allow organizations to function easily, instantly and over any distance. They allow independence from corporate publishing companies and break the confines of geography. The problem is, anyone can start a group or write a book. Self-proclaimed experts continually add to the heaps of rubbish that confuse more than they clarify. The true power of rare, secretive, texts is vanishing. Productions like the Azoetia and the Viridarium Umbris represent the last of books that contain power beyond the written words that they contain. Individuals can start occult organizations very easily with the help of the technology at our disposal. The Seeker must devote so much of his/her time in order to find something worth while that they have little time left to apply these worth while findings to their personal development.

Is the Order of the Voltec one of these useless groups created by self proclaimed "experts"? Are the materials produced by the Order of the Voltec to be added to the piles of tomes that merely repeat Regardie, LaVey, Aquino, Carroll, Hines, Cunningham, etc? Maybe. The Seeker is hereby asked to spend just a little more time before giving up entirely. Read this text and make a decision based on your own expertise and knowledge without being asked to take my, or anyone else's word for it.

So if the Internet and "print on demand" technology is aiding the decline of worthwhile materials, why did the Order of the Voltec decide to use this method for this publication? As I had stated earlier in this chapter, these technologies are really a two edged sword. This text is to provide the interested individual with a glimpse into our little group. While it is true that we make no attempts to recruit new members or try to convince people that our system is the "best", we do feel that an individual, with a good amount of curiosity should be given a chance to assess the Order of the Voltec in order to determine if this book falls into the .05% of sincere and worth while attempts of development of the Self.

To go further into our theories and practices would require an examination of our other texts, such as, The Book of the Black Amber, the Downward Path into Nod, Twilight Undone and the Sorcery of Perception. Unfortunately, for the Seeker, a "good amount of curiosity" isn't enough to acquire these materials. The Seeker is, in this case, out of luck. The Order of the Voltec believes such texts are Power Objects in, and of, themselves. Talismanic Publications are our standard. We hand make each volume in very limited numbers and make them available only to Active Members in good standing. In this way our texts amount to more than the sum of the words between the covers. These are items of Power that come to life when the Seeker reads them and consciously puts the information contained therein into use. Very few texts will be made available through "print on demand" sources, but the Seeker, whom chooses to go beyond mere "curiosity", is welcome to apply for active membership (Active Membership is discussed in the "Affiliation and Admissions Policies" chapter).

Our work imbues Power and it takes a monumental effort. This text is designed to, briefly, describe what a "Voltec" is, what the Order of the Voltec seeks to accomplish and how the organization itself is setup.

Good Luck Fellow Seekers,

Deus Factus Sum,

Wendigo V°
Voice of the Downward Path

Introduction

I was looking over several of my old magical journals, pondering those many years of discovery and change that had lead up to this very moment. My earliest recollections of childhood are filled with my internal opposition to the bright and irritating world into which I was born. When I was about four years old, I remember that a collection of drawings that I had done had suddenly disappeared. The drawings were of demonic beings with horns and forked tongues. They were drawn on colored construction paper. I vaguely remember confronting my parents about my beloved creatures and knowing that they had gotten rid of them. This was to be representative of the struggle that I was to both endure and pledge myself to for the rest of my life. When I received my first camera at the age of seven, my parents were quite dismayed when they picked up the roll of developed film and found a stack of photos with nothing on them but pictures of tomb stones from a colonial cemetery in Massachusetts. From the moment I could think, my thoughts revolved turbulently around witchcraft, the dead and anything having to do with the twilight realms to which I instinctively felt I belonged. My upbringing was nothing extraordinary. My parent's were highly successful professionals and I was raised as a well off white Catholic boy.

On my first Halloween when I was old enough to choose what I wanted to be, I demanded that I go trick or treating as a witch. Of course I couldn't be a witch. Witches were girls. I was a boy. I went as a witch. My mother even made an orange wig out of a mop head so I could sport long red hair. I think that I wanted to be a witch every year, but settled for other costumes out of sheer aggravation. For several years when I was growing up I begged my parents to let me have Halloween theme parties for my birthday, which was in August. They conceded. After all, I was just a child. What was there to worry about?

The adolescent years are always such a delight, both for the individual going through that transition and for those around them who must endure the stormier upheavals associated with that time. A second resurgence of the popular new age movement was just starting, and their were precious few places to procure the reading materials that I was drawn to. When I was a child, Fairy tales and monster movies satisfied me for the time, but as I grew and my world view began to expand, I craved new sources of stimulation. Like so many of us, I scraped together a few dollars and bought a copy of the cheap paperback edition of the Necronomicon that was available at the local mall book stores at that time. I memorized the names of the elder gods and the old ones, and fantasized about invoking the watchers at night in the forest. I used to sneak out of my house on breezy fall nights and congregate with the few friends that I had. We would spend our time making small fires in the woods and trying to summon elemental spirits. It was on one of these nights that, black robed I knelt down before a full moon and whispered my allegiances to the powers of the night. A friend who stood a few feet behind me watched as the wind blew and lifted my satiny black cape and said "you're a sorcerer," as if he had just discovered something forbidden. That was the truth. My truth. My friend had said it without thinking, and it rang true to the core of my adolescent being. I did not outwardly acknowledge what my friend said that night, but I think back on it and smile. Those words framed a feeling for me that would grow until it would become a consuming fire, and eventually change the actual fabric of what I am as a sentient being. The night, the moon and the wind quenched an almost painful thirst that I had always had and those words "you are a sorcerer," validated something in me that could not be validated in any other way or on any other occasion. The darkness itself reached out to me and embraced the truth that could not be thought about as one is accustomed to thinking about things. This kind of truthfulness exists beyond values and it is what people crave most, yet work so hard at hiding from. I was a sorcerer. I did not have any truly developed sense of what that meant, but it would become the guiding force of my life from them on. I would become moved by something that would remain always just out of sight, changing and fluid yet potent, intelligent and beyond time.

Magic, mysticism and obscure religions became a daily obsession, and I scoured libraries, used book stores and the collections of friends who had already spent time devoted to the dark arts. When I was a senior in high school, I spent a few days in study hall reading the Avon paperback edition of the Satanic Bible. This was a work that I could truly immerse myself in. It excited me in a way that other works only hinted at. As an angry teen about to be loosed upon a hypocritical materialistic society, I embraced LaVey's dark genius and began to incorporate the ideas set forth in that satanic tomb into my teen angst belief system. I did not strictly adhere to the principles of Satanism. I was, after all not looking for concrete answers concerning the world in which I lived. I was not searching for an adversarial code to live by, but I was fascinated with Satanism's exaltation of the carnal and its sense of dark glamour. I also enjoyed the simplicity with which Anton LaVey approached ritual magic. This approach allowed the witch or warlock to realistically perform black magic without having to travel to distant lands in order to gather rare ingredients for some ancient folk spell. I gathered together some rudimentary ritual components and set up a small satanic alter in my bedroom. Now, I had been engaged in a constant struggle with my worried parents since I was a child regarding my true interests and magical tendencies. There had been many times when I would find books or incense that I had hidden missing from their secret places. I had become proficient at keeping my obsessions and their bounty well hidden from the view of the people who were better off not knowing. My satanic alter was easily set up and taken down at will, and I housed my ritual supplies and implements inside of the marble topped, hard wood cabinet that became magically transformed when I desired. All I had to do was throw my shiny black alter cloth over the table, and viola it was now a portal of energy and a common meeting place for me and the powers of darkness. At this point in time I had no idea that affiliation with the popularly despised Church of Satan (COS) was possible, and I had no inkling that the Temple of Set even existed. I was a young, virile warlock bustling with electricity and I was more concerned with what my own powers could bring me in terms of lust and the satisfaction of my baser wants. I had a few friends with which to affiliate who had similar interests to mine, and this curbed any natural craving for contact with others. I was not organized in the sense that a mature black magician should be, but I learned to rely on the power of magic. At the drop of a hat I would mold a voluptuous waxen image and anoint in with my hot, freshly spent semen. I would write down my enemies name and seal it in a glass vial containing an assortment of undesirable elements. What kept me hooked and moving forward on the path of sorcery was that things would happen when I worked my spells, often in unexpected ways, but things would happen with enough regularity to strengthen my beliefs and even cause me to develop a greater respect for the powers that I was youthfully tampering with. It began to dawn on me that there were highly intelligent forces behind the appearances of every day life and that these forces, when beckoned would respond without any hesitation at all. I began to have dreams where I would find myself in ancient cemeteries and rotting old houses surrounded by an ever changing array of exotic entities. Tornadoes became a very common theme in my sleeping state, and eventually I began to keep dream journals in order to try and find some intelligible pattern of meaning in my nightly excursions. The practice of magic and my dreaming experiences led me to explore every avenue of occult literature that I could manage. I absorbed every book on witchcraft that I could find and eventually discovered the works of the great beast himself, Aleister Crowley. Crowley's Magick was deeper than anything I had previously been exposed to. Questions that I had come up with were somehow answered in the context of his system. Of course! It was so easy to understand. Magick was the art and science of causing change to occur in conformity with one's will. Everything we did as conscious beings was, in some way magickal. Through Crowley, I was introduced to other occult personalities such as Israel Regardie and Dion Fortune. This exposure was, of course how I became acquainted with the Holy Kabala. Here was an ancient mystical diagram of the secret workings of the universe. The anatomy of the body of God, handed down through the Hebrew mystics and reinterpreted by the most devoted and knowledgeable sorcerers of the time. I diligently memorized the Hebrew alphabet, and their correspondences on the tree of life and I began to take the practice of Magick to a new level where self discipline would help me hone skills of concentration and creative imagination. I bought and read every piece of Crowley's work that I could get my hands on. I also studied the Kabala and sought self initiation through the system employed by the OTO. At one time I did have the fortunate experience of dating a gorgeous blonde member of that organization, and I was initiated to the degree of minerval in New York City, but I was not yet at the point where I could make a solid commitment to such a renown occult order, and in time I lost contact. I dedicated my personal time to perfecting Crowley's pentagram rituals, performing basic yoga and attempting to familiarize myself with the astral plane. I delved into the Enochian system and memorized verses from Liber Al Vel Legis. New age occult book stores were abundant at this time, and it was not difficult to befriend other like minded individuals while browsing through the newest editions. I had a small group of Thelemite friends, and we kept each other relatively busy discussing our thoughts on the Aeon of the crowned and conquering child and Aiwass.

There was, underneath the flow of my education in magic, the pervasive influence of a certain author that I had slowly become acquainted with over the years. When I was in high school, a friend had recommended a small paperback book entitled the Teachings of Don Juan, a Yaqui Way of Knowledge, by Carlos Castaneda. I read the little tomb, Enjoying the talk about powerful brujos and corn sorcery, but somehow none of it really stuck. The one part of the work that eventually brought me back to Castaneda's writing was the segment where, aided by the "little smoke" and the guidance of Don Juan, Castaneda turned into a crow. It took years before I sat down and read a Separate Reality and Journey to Ixtlan. By that time I was ready to let go of some of the rigid practices that I had relied upon as my magical foundation and began to open up to the possibilities experienced by Castaneda during his initiation into Toltec sorcery. I started to understand that to rely on absolute concepts in the realm of the dark arts was tantamount to active hypocrisy.

The arch angels and angels of the Tree of Life had always and would always be there, perfect in their divine geometry. The Tree would go unchanged, as the spheres continually emanate their share of the omnipotent flux of Divine Will. The pentagrams would always be erected, and the circles cast to protect the magician from the winds that rage on outside, but at the end of the Aeon, nothing would change, least of all the lone wizard clinging to his wand and cup wondering where all the magick had gone.

Castaneda's books cannot be read once and internalized in the way that one would read a work of fiction, or even a historical biography. Each time I have read one of them, new features of a strange landscape would emerge. Things that I did not see the first time would appear, as if my own Awareness at the time of reading would cause new perceptions and realizations to become possible. The more I read and reread, the more the world of the ancient Toltec opened up and beckoned to me from a place far away and thousands of years in the past. I never became a Castaneda fanatic. I did not follow him across the country and attend his "Tensegrity" seminars. In fact, all I really did was continue on my path, reading and rereading his work. Eventually I started putting into practice those things about which the Toltec Seer wrote. At first I wanted the world of Castaneda's sorcery to open up to my beckoning, and with a little work I began to see concrete and pragmatic results. There are a few basic ideas which originate in Castaneda's work, that I must acquaint the reader with before I can discuss Toltec sorcery's relevance to the Left Hand Path.

Carlos Castaneda was indoctrinated into an all inclusive realm of cognition entirely different from the one we are familiar with. He was acted upon by sorcerers who were intimately familiar with this other reality, and he was slowly groomed to the point where he could interact independently both in the sorcerer's world and the world of every day affairs. The sorcerers of this Toltec lineage maintain that one's perception of the world is only a description that has been handed down to them by their ancestors and social predecessors. Castaneda explains that from the minute we are born into this world, our perception is molded by the adults around us until one day it resembles the perception of those same individuals, our teachers. When we are children we perceive in a way that is almost alien to us as adults. We visually see in very different ways and we interact with the universe based off of our raw Awareness. As we grow , we are coached to perceive the world in concrete terms that have been established within the accepted social milieu. For a child, a boulder becomes a boulder when the child accepts it as such. Up until this point, a boulder is a sensory adventure. When we give something a name and learn about its most humanly relevant qualities, we then have a tendency to group it together with other things that resemble it, and to categorize it according to how important it is to us. This is the social part of perception that Castaneda talks about so much.

You may now be wondering what this has to do with the Left Hand Path and sorcery in general. Well, by the end of this chapter I promise that it will become clear.

The key to our perception is also the key to our Power. The Toltec sorcerers, through their practices discovered that in order to make real changes in the world and in ourselves, we had to first shift our perception away from the description of the world into which we had been indoctrinated from our birth. They spoke of a realm of activity called the "Second Attention," where all that we did not immediately perceive existed independent of our human knowledge. Practically speaking, the Second Attention is everything that exists in the multi-verse that we normally do not have the capability to perceive directly.

When I was a child, I had a keen interest in all kinds of art. I could always be found engaged in some type of creative act whether it was painting or fabricating something out of junk that I found in the garage. I still remember something very interesting about my acts of creativity as a child. During art class in school I would often become so involved in the project that I was working on that everything else around me would disappear. I literally remember the sounds of the other children and the classroom fading out to somewhere far in the background. I can remember that my body would feel almost rigid and that time would seem to speed up to an astonishing rate. When the class was over, I would have to take a few minutes to adjust back to the regular classroom environment. It was almost exactly like waking up from a deep sleep, as I would have to stretch my body out and let my vision adjust to the commotion around me. I understand now that I had been somewhere else. My concentration had been total, and I was wholly engaged in one single act. As we grow up and the concerns of the world become our concerns, this sharp ability to focus our awareness seems to disappear little by little. I have studied children, and they all have this capacity to concentrate completely on what they are doing. As we age, we are socialized to expect some type of reward for our actions, and we loose the ability to play and interact as children do. There is something very interesting about this type of concentration we have and experience as children. It is total. Time not only seems to fly, it does fly and this demonstrates the fact that time is the perceivable byproduct of attention. Time is perceived to flow according to the quality of attention of the perceiver. When grown-ups experience this type of one-pointed attention they either forget about it or call it meditation, and the reason that we do it naturally as children is because we are not yet filled to the brim with social worries and concerns. We are born with this capacity to concentrate because it is essential to our well-being. The question is why do we so easily loose this ability as we get older? Every day, as we grow, our minds and, in turn, our energy become less and less our own.

The essence of the Left Hand Path is individuality, not absorption. I do not want you to confuse the Left Hand Path concept of individuality with the human compulsion of self absorption, or self importance. Every time we adopt and internalize one of our parents or society's beliefs about the world as our own, we limit our future ability to perceive in a freer manner. We begin to interpret the world in terms of a set social and perceptual consensus. What do I mean by this? I mean that the whole of our reality is structured on principles and ideas that we have agreed to, or have been forced to believe in. If our parents felt that a person's worth stemmed mostly from how much money they made, we more than likely will adopt this belief as our own, and it will exist at some level of predominance in our awareness. The Toltec sorcerers understood that we were taught what to perceptually emphasize, and in turn what to perceptually value. Therefore, what we place emphasis on becomes the confines of our reality. All else is skimmed over and fades into the background. This shadow realm is where our true power lays, waiting for us to beckon it. This shadow realm is the second attention, or what we call the nightside.

There came a time, after years of putting Toltec principles into practice, when these concepts began to resonate strongly with what I had learned about Black Magic and the Left Hand Path. Toltec sorcery gave new life to everything I had learned about the dark side if initiation and it also opened doors to understanding Left Hand Path sorcery with a new type of depth. There is a world of difference between reading and understanding a principle of magic, and actually experiencing the effects of sorcery in the objective world. Fusing together my earliest knowledge with the fundamentals of Left Hand Path sorcery and the techniques of the Toltec's eventually allowed me to discover far reaching power outside of the ritual chamber, and to put into practice that which is usually only fantasized about.

Iremoch VI°
Voice of the Backwards Way

What is "Voltec"?

The term "Voltec" is a composite word from two root words; "Voltigeur" (Leapers on the Reverse Side of the Tree of Life) and "Toltec". These two terms are the basis of what a Voltec "is" and describe how s/he does it, therefore deserve some initial explanation.

The Voltigeur are described, somewhat, by the noted occultist, Kenneth Grant. He claims that the Voltigeur is a term used by Black Snake cultists to denote leapers or vaulters on the reverse side of the Tree of Life. The Frog and Bat are the totems of these Leapers (hence the OV frogbat logo). As the reader will come to learn, we use the Tree of Life, the Reverse Side of the Tree of Life (Typhonian Tree) and the, Voltec specific, Tree of Night (see the chapter on the Tree of Night). Iremoch VI° has informed the Order of the Voltec, through his writing, that the term Voltigeur also is used in Haitian Voodoo to describe a sorcerer that employs Black Magic. In an article that was published when the Order of the Voltec was still an element within the Temple of Set (see "History of the Order of the Voltec) Iremoch VI° states, *"the Voltec is a Voltigeur because they regard each perceptual mode as a platform, from which they strive to leap to the next perceptual mode..."* (Journal of the Silver Twilight 1999).

The second element, from which our composite name comes, "Toltec" has been written about by New Age authors for decades but the Toltec system is best described within the works of Carlos Castaneda. The Order of the Voltec has chosen his representation of the Toltec system because it provides an energetic framework, over which any magical system or technique may be placed because the Toltec system does not impose any cultural or belief system whatsoever. *"The Toltec system is expressly concerned with the expansion of Awareness through the modification and, willful, manipulation of Perception"* (Iremoch VI° 1999).

"There came a time, after years of putting Toltec principles into practice, when these concepts began to resonate strongly with what I had learned about black magic and the Left Hand Path. Toltec sorcery gave new life to everything I had learned about the dark side of initiation and it also opened doors to understanding Left Hand Path sorcery with a new type of depth. There is a world of difference between reading and understanding a principle of magic, and actually experiencing the effects of sorcery in the objective world. Fusing together my earliest knowledge with the fundamentals of Left Hand Path sorcery and the techniques of the Toltecs eventually allowed me to discover far reaching power outside of the ritual chamber, and to put into practice that which is usually only fantasized about". (Iremoch VI°).

There are numerous influences that helps to shape what a Voltec is to become. The concepts of the Voltigeur and of the Toltec Shaman are but two of the more prevalent. Of course, it is beyond the scope of this brief introduction to the ideas of the Voltec to discuss all of these influences. The potential Voltec Sorcerer is encouraged to create a unique framework, upon which, these ideas may be placed in such a way that they can be utilized as a Point of Departure.

History and Evolution of the Order of the Voltec

The founding members of the Order of the Voltec had met during their membership in another Left Hand Path organization called the Temple of Set. Unless you are extremely new to the occult world, I am sure you already know of the Temple of Set, therefore, not much will be explained about that particular group. The Temple of Set is mentioned only to clarify how the Order of the Voltec came into being as it stands today.

In 1996, within the Temple of Set, the co-founders of the Order of the Voltec formed a regional group referred to as a "Pylon" (ToS equivalent of a CoS "Grotto"). We opened this Pylon to non-regional members as well and as a result, the Pylon of the Voltigeur attracted members seeking to integrate the ideas of Carlos Castaneda into the their personal program.

"Our pylon instantly attracted a few members from different locations across the country, and we soon published our first formalized journal for circulation within the ToS. The Pylon of the Voltigeur came into being in order to aid the interested Setian in their search for new areas of black magical exploration. As the co-creator of this small group, I felt that it was my primary obligation to actively oppose the element of stagnation that one is bound to confront as an adept of the Left Hand Path. The guiding principles of this pylon were formulated based off of the understanding that a black magician needed to be in a constant state of willingness to transcend their own limitations". (Iremoch VI°)

The Pylon of the Voltigeur produced "The Journal of the Silver Twilight" which we intended to release on a bi-monthly basis to inform the rest of the ToS what we were working on. The Journal of the Silver Twilight was not well received by the ToS, for whatever reason, and eventually the co-creators decided to take their experience and ideas to a new level. They talked extensively about how important taking action was for the Left Hand Path initiate, instead of simply day dreaming about wicked practices and world domination. They had experienced real, concrete results with the forms of sorcery that they were working with, and wanted to begin sharing this with other interested individuals. The Pylon of the Voltigeur had appealed to certain Setians who were interested in, or had personal experience combining Toltec practices, shamanism, chaos magic and other diverse approaches to the unknown. Eventually the Order of the Voltec emerged as the next phase in the evolution of Left Hand Path consciousness.

This evolution, of LHP organizations, maps out the Energetic flow the early days of the Church of Satan, through the current manifestation of the Temple of Set to the specific application principles of the Order of the Voltec.

The CoS was the beginning of the process of self discovery. A decadent religious and societal rebellion, orchestrated at the right time in the right place. It succeeded in temporarily liberating the awareness of its members and re-fortifying the image of the LHP with dark Satanic purpose. Their philosophies were contradictory and lead the CoS to outright and exaggerated dysfunction. The Church of Satan focused on the concept of "Indulgence". During that time, indulgence was not at all a foreign topic (the sexual revolution was at its peak and experimentation with mind altering substances was becoming a national past time) however, Anton LaVey presented Indulgence in a context that was still taboo at that time. Using shock value and pseudo-occult atmospheres, LaVey, unknowingly, facilitated a release of static energies in the members of the CoS. The liberation of energies is an important step in personal development but it cannot be considered an ultimate goal. Because LaVey did not provide an environment where the members of the CoS could utilize these liberated energies for perceptual purposes, they (the CoS) merely reinvested these energies into their social gatherings held in the guise of ritual. All serious LHP occultists will outgrow the goals of the CoS, which becomes evident when one reads the Satanic Bible, which will always be the first and most important book of its kind. Nothing in the CoS changed and the more occult oriented individuals (with subjective goals) began to, unknowingly, seek a "use" for their newly liberated energies as well as a non-ordinary consciousness. These members ultimately did leave the CoS to form the second LHP organization of concern, The Temple of Set.

In 1975 the Church of Satan's highest ranking member (other than LaVey), Michael Aquino, formed the Temple of Set. I can't claim to know all of the reasons that caused these members of the CoS to resign, however, this split was a result of the CoS refusing to change. It was in this organization (the ToS) that the founding members of the Order of the Voltec met and began working together. The ToS has a system which allows its members to pursue Setian interests and form regional groups known as "pylons" (which are similar to the COS "grottos"). The Pylon of the Voltigeur was created as a vehicle for Setians to pursue their initiation using the systems and techniques described by Carlos Castaneda and Kenneth Grant (neither of these two writers are looked upon in a positive way by the ToS). This pylon turned out to be an unrefined version of the Order of the Voltec that exists today. The TOS focuses on an Egyptian concept known as Xeper, which means "Becoming", "To Become", or "Come into Being". This, like Indulgence, is a necessary step but cannot be an ultimate goal either. Becoming was a valid employment for those liberated energies but will also be outgrown in most cases.

So what is the ultimate goal? With the birth of the Temple Of Set, the LHP saw an invigorated new beginning, as well as an intellectualized re-defining. It is with the ToS that the LHP became a true school of modern philosophy and black magic. As former members of the ToS, we do not wish to denounce it in any way, however, if we are to be truthful in re-defining the LHP, then comparisons must be made until understanding has been achieved. The ToS defines the LHP as: *"The conscious attempt to preserve and strengthen one's isolate, psyche centric existence against the objective universe while apprehending, comprehending, and influencing a varying number of subjective universes."* **The OV defines the LHP as: "The willful liberation and re-deployment of one's personal energy for the purpose of entering into the left-field (Nightside) of Awareness".** This effort implies everything that the ToS definition contains, but it is an extension and living challenge to act, not simply speculate.

The Voltec liberates and re-deploys their existing energy through the use of non-ordinary techniques in order to experience greater perceptual possibilities. This liberated energy is further utilizes in the continued expansion of awareness. We regard the Left-field or the Nightside of attention as that vast ocean of perceptual options within our reach, yet inaccessible through ordinary means.

So, through this process of organizational evolution, the Order of the Voltec has sought these "greater perceptual possibilities" through various means.

The Order of the Voltec was formed after the realization was made that further evolutionary steps must be taken. The founding members of the Order of the Voltec structured this organization in 1999 and began to continually refine the principles, practices and theories that govern it. After seven years of refinement the Order of the Voltec opened its doors to other individuals interested in seeking the same changes that so many others have for thousands of years.

The Order of the Voltec is the next step (and final step) in the Energetic Evolution of the Left Hand Path. The OV stresses a focus on becoming fluid and cultivating an awareness of perceptual states. This we know to be the last goal while retaining form in the First Attention (physical embodiment). Any subsequent steps to be taken hereafter cannot be pursued within any occult organization; therefore the ultimate goal of a Voltec initiate is Departure from the Human Form and the total mastery of perception and awareness.

The history of the Order of the Voltec extends back many centuries, back to the times of ancient Sorcerers. Each time an expression of these ideas pushes itself into manifestation, the process becomes a little clearer. We are in very exciting times. A time when we have so much information available and methods in place to use it. No matter the cultural context nor the time era of creation, the Voltec has, at his/her disposal, all of these tools in which s/he can pursue the process of Self Deification.

Carlos Castaneda and the Core Concepts

I am sure that it is obvious, by now, that the Order of the Voltec draws heavily upon the terms and ideas presented in the books written by Carlos Castaneda. At this point, I think it is imperative that I make a few points clear. The Order of the Voltec does not wish to debate the issue of whether Castaneda actually experienced the things that he wrote about in his books, we do not care if there "really" was a don Juan Matus, we do not seek an answer to the fiction or non-fiction question surrounding his work. Such speculations draw people's attentions away from the true value of Castaneda's work.

The Order of the Voltec does not use the principles that are presented in the Castaneda texts in the same ways as they are originally presented, nor does it take the Castaneda texts as its "bible". The characters and events described, while interesting and entertaining vehicles, are secondary to the OV's application of Castaneda's concepts. The Voltec is asked to filter out the non-essential elements in these works and to focus on the "core concepts".

The value of Castaneda's work, in the eyes of the Order of the Voltec, was his ability to identify, describe and define the more elusive elements of magick that have escaped occult groups altogether for centuries. These concepts include; erasing personal history, using Death as the prime motivator of action, becoming inaccessible to undesirable influences, losing self importance, dissolving debilitating habits, silencing the internal dialogue and many more.

Some of the Core Concepts that a Voltec Initiate will need to become familiar with are listed and briefly described below. Please be aware that this is a partial list and the Core Concepts of Castaneda are far reaching and influence nearly all aspects of the Voltec process. Detailed descriptions, examples and exercises pertaining to the principles are provided in *Energetic Sorcery on the Voltec Tree of Night* (Wendigo V° 2008 Voltec Publishing).

Controlled Folly: This concept is the acknowledgment that our actions have little importance in the larger scheme of things. We realize what we do doesn't really matter, but we act as though it does. This concept prevents performing actions and expecting specific results. The actions may then be undertaken for their own value and not for the accumulated results of those actions.

Cognitive Dissonance: The intentional breaking of patterns and placing of ones self into uncomfortable situations. The Voltec Initiate knows that maintaining patterns utilizes a large amount of personal energy and breaking such patterns frees this energy to be used for other purposes.

Losing Self Importance: Self Importance, not to be confused with the Left Hand Path concept of individuality, is the human compulsion of self absorption. Self Importance interferes with how effective we are in the applications of our Sorcery. The Voltec must learn to not take him/herself too seriously.

Living Beyond Consensual Reality: Living beyond Consensual Reality is breaking the patterns that society has imposed on an individual. Much like breaking personal patterns using Cognitive Dissonance, forming a new, non-ordinary, consensus is deeply important. This is the importance of a LHP Initiate joining a group despite the LHP process being so individualistic. The OV serves as a new Consensual Reality in which the Sorcerer finds Freedom of Perception without others forcing an agreement of "Reality" upon the practitioner.

Detachment: Detachment helps the Voltec adapt to the instabilities of life. They learn to use Death as an Advisor so that they treat every action as though it is there last.

Silencing the Internal Dialogue: The Internal Dialogue is the constant chatter in our heads. Humans endlessly talk to themselves through Internal Dialogue and, in doing so, define "reality". If we acquire the ability to temporarily suspend the Internal Dialogue, the Voltec can "Stop the World" and perceive entirely new aspects of Reality.

Erasing Personal History: Don Juan tells Castaneda… *"If you have no personal history, no explanations are needed; nobody is angry or disillusioned with your acts. And above all no one pins you down with their thoughts."* The Voltec Initiate eliminates the distribution of personal information to other individuals. Through various means the remnants of their Personal History is dismantled piece by piece.

These examples are demonstrative of simple ideas that can make a world of difference to any magician, Voltec or otherwise. One of the most important of the Core Concepts, not dealt with above, is the focus of the next chapter. The concept of the Assemblage Point, in my opinion, is Castaneda's greatest contribution to the occult and therefore I have decided to include an entire section of this text on its explanation. In the following chapter, Iremoch VI° clearly explains this all important concept.

The Assemblage Point

One of the most important concepts that the Voltec has adopted from the discoveries of the ancient Toltec sorcerers, and from the works of Carlos Castaneda, is the "Assemblage Point." The ancient Toltec sorcerers perceived, through their dreaming, that the human organism was composed of the physical, material body as well as a field of energy which surrounds and encases the human body. This shell of energy extends for a considerable distance around our physical selves, and it houses many energetic configurations (similar to the idea of energy Chakras) that are, under ordinary circumstances, unperceivable to our five senses. The Toltec sorcerers perceived that our basic nature is rooted in this energetic field, which is in turn vitally connected to the energy configuration of the universe at large. The most important single feature of our energy field is a chakra-like energy center the Toltecs called the assemblage point.

In his work, The Fire From Within (1984), Castaneda passes on to us the explanations that his sorcery teacher elaborated for him, concerning the Assemblage Point and Awareness. *"He briefly outlined the truths about awareness he had discussed: that there is no objective world, but only a universe of energy fields which Seers call the Eagle's emanations. That human beings are made out of the Eagle's emanations and are in essence bubbles of luminescent energy; each of us is wrapped in a cocoon that encloses a small portion of these emanations. That awareness is achieved by the constant pressure that the emanations outside of our cocoons, which are called emanations at large, exert on those inside our cocoons. That awareness gives rise to perception, which happens when the emanations inside our cocoons align themselves with the corresponding emanations at large."* (108) Concerning the assemblage point he says in The Art of Dreaming (1993), *" In the course of his teachings, don Juan repeatedly discussed and explained what he considered the decisive finding of the sorcerers of antiquity. He called it the crucial feature of human beings as luminous balls: a round spot of intense brilliance, the size of a tennis ball, permanently lodged inside the luminous ball, flush with its surface, about two feet back from the crest of a person's right shoulder blade."* This is what the ancient Toltec sorcerers called the "Assemblage Point," he goes on to say, *" The old sorcerers saw that, in human beings, perception is assembled there, on that point."* Now, the ancient Toltec sorcerers conceived of the universe as being composed of an infinite number of luminous thread-like filament structures, which extend into forever in every conceivable direction. *"For such sorcerers, the most significant act of sorcery is to see the essence of the universe. Don Juan's version was that the sorcerers of antiquity, the first ones to see the essence of the universe, described it in the best manner. They said that the essence of the universe resembles incandescent threads stretched into infinity in every conceivable direction, luminous filaments that are conscious of themselves in ways impossible for the human mind to comprehend."* The Assemblage Point creates sensory data from the luminous threads that pass directly through it. Thus, our world is created by the Assemblage Point, and the habitual position to which it is fixed. The Assemblage Point is an energy center that has, as its sole purpose, turning the fluctuating energy of the universe into perceivable units of data. Human beings Assemblage Points are all generally located on the same positions on their energy cocoons. This common positioning is the reason all human beings perceive the world in relatively the same way.

It has been a large task of the Order of the Voltec to liberate Castaneda's work from the "New Age" movement and the destructive drug culture that gravitate to these texts. We have made a large effort to take these principles and redefine them and place them within a practical context that will be of use to the Left Hand Path Initiate. The "Not Doings" described in Castaneda's books are an excellent example of directly applicable theories for the Black Magician. A Not Doing is an unlearning process whereby the Voltec Initiate unravels assumed roles and descriptions used to define "reality". In order to entertain these new perceptions the Voltec must assign equal value to both the physical world and the Shadow Realm.

All Initiates of the Order of the Voltec are expected to become familiar with the "Core Concepts" and how they can be deployed in their quest for Self Deification. The majority of the I° work is geared towards understanding the Core Concepts and providing examples of their applications.

"There is a world of difference between reading and understanding a principle of magic, and actually experiencing the effects of sorcery in the objective world. Fusing together my earliest knowledge with the fundamentals of Left Hand Path sorcery and the techniques of the Toltecs eventually allowed me to discover far reaching power outside of the ritual chamber, and to put into practice that which is usually only fantasized about" (Iremoch VI°)

The key to all sorcery, as discovered by the Toltecs, is that the Assemblage Point can move, and when it does, whole new realms of real perception become available. What keeps the Assemblage Point locked in place is the power of habituation. Our cultivated familiarity about the world is like a weight that keeps the Assemblage Point from moving. The tighter the lock down, the more worldly and reasonable the person is likely to be. The paramount discovery of the Toltec sorcerers was that the Assemblage Point could be made to move. A second discovery of incredible magnitude was that, once moved, the Assemblage Point could be made to stay on its new position, thus granting the sorcerer an entirely new and steady perception. When the Assemblage Point moves erratically, perception is clouded and just as erratic. It takes the Assemblage Point resting on one place for a time in order to render a steady perception of the new energetic configuration. Along with the discoveries about the Assemblage Point, came the knowledge that the underlying energetic structure of the universe is perceivable by human beings under certain perceptual conditions. These conditions resemble dream states to a great degree. The Toltecs found that the Assemblage Point could be made to move through behaviors that were considered extreme or uncharacteristic. Since our normal way of thinking and behaving is what keeps the Assemblage Point in its place, then it makes sense that acting outside of our comfortable boundaries would cause a shift in the assemblage point. Extreme hunger, elation, fear or fatigue are but a few of the conditions that the ancient sorcerers subjected themselves to in order to break the boundaries of consensual awareness. The ingestion of hallucinogenic plants was another. The ancient Toltec sorcerers used ritual techniques to move their attention away from the ordinary, and then purposely induced the movement of the Assemblage Point in order to catch a glimpse into other dimensions.

The next major discovery of the Toltec sorcerers was that the Assemblage Point also moves by itself, naturally during sleep. They perceived, in states of deep dream like meditation, that while sleeping, the Assemblage Points of human beings naturally moved. This movement was discovered to be directly connected to dreaming. Either dreaming caused the Assemblage Point to move, or the Assemblage Points moving resulted in dreaming. Because of this naturally occurring movement, the Toltec sorcerers began to explore ways that they could experiment with, and utilize it. According to Castaneda, this is how the Art of Dreaming was born. The ancient Toltec sorcerers developed the ability to become fully conscious and aware at the level of dreaming, and through this talent, they also discovered that the conditions of a human beings world were entirely dependant on the position of the Assemblage Point. Through their dreaming practices, they also found out that other, real and all encompassing worlds existed other than just the world of every day affairs.

The Assemblage Point moves as a result of drastic, unusual circumstances and behaviors, or as a result of the natural flow of the dreaming that we all experience while asleep. The natural conclusion that the Toltec sorcerers came to with regard to this knowledge, was that when the Assemblage Point did move, the resulting perception of the individual sorcerer would be incomprehensible to them, unless the Assemblage Point could be made to stay put on its new position. If this could be achieved, the human capacity to interpret sensory data with the five senses would kick in, and a new version of reality would be come perceivable.

Castaneda says in The Fire From Within, *"Seers see that infants have no fixed Assemblage Point at first. Their encased emanations are in a state of great turmoil, and their Assemblage Points shift everywhere in the band of man, giving children a great capacity to focus on emanations that later will be thoroughly disregarded. Then as they grow, the older humans around them, through their considerable power over them, force the children's Assemblage Points to become steadier by means of an increasingly complex internal dialogue. The internal dialogue is a process that constantly strengthens the position of the Assemblage Point, because that position is an arbitrary one and needs steady reinforcement."* One can now easily see why sorcerers indulge in long bouts of silence and seemingly strange behavior. It is all with a purpose in mind and that purpose it to become physically, perceptually and energetically fluid. This happens when the sorcerer learns how to move their Assemblage Points. Heightened Awareness, trances, spiritual experiences and visions are all the result of such a movement. The Voltec Sorcerer uses the conception of the Assemblage Point in order to systematically enter into the Nightside. The very nature of the Assemblage Point makes it a very difficult concept to deal with. When we feel most content and firmly grounded, the Assemblage Point is strongly fixed at its habitual position. This explains so much about the frightening nature of sorcery. The natural fixation of the Assemblage Point, demands that the individual leaves the comfort of their daily routine if they have any hope of breaking their perceptual boundaries.

The use of drugs to alter perception is, understandably, a convenient alternative for fasting or subjecting one's self to frightening experiences. With drugs and hallucinogens, we have the safety of knowing that the drug will wear off eventually. We know that as long as we are relatively safe, our minds will remain intact. Unfortunately, the Toltec sorcerers who used hallucinogenic plants as a doorway to the Nightside, ultimately became completely dependant on them for this purpose. There are other ways to achieve non-ordinary states without subjecting oneself to the risk of death or insanity.

Do not simply accept what Castaneda has written about this detrimental topic. I didn't, but after many years of experience, I can not deny the concept of the Assemblage Point. It is a phenomenon to be experienced, just like dreaming or any other facet of the Voltec sorcerer's world. Once experienced, the Assemblage Point becomes a reasonable proposition. Once it is experienced again and again, it becomes a fundamental part of our vast potential as creatures who posses awareness. A sorcerer is one who has discovered the Assemblage Point and has willfully made it move. This can happen in many ways, each a personal expression of the sorcerer in question, but the moment that is happens, the ordinary person is forever transformed into something else.

The Tree of Night

The Order of the Voltec often refers to concepts like, the Assemblage Point, Positions of the Assemblage Point, Shifting and Moving the Assemblage Point, the Tree of Night, Power Zones (a.k.a. Sephiroth) of the Tree of Night and the Tunnels of Set. These terms and the concepts they represent are vital for successful applications of the Voltec system. This section will serve as a valuable reference for anyone who intends on using any materials the Order of the Voltec issues.

Assemblage Point

The first concept that is absolutely necessary to comprehend is the Assemblage Point (see the previous chapter for Iremoch's excellent overview). As with most schools of magic or mystical systems, the Order of the Voltec acknowledges the existence of the Energy Body, which we call the Shadow Self. This Shadow Self is the focus of our goals of Immortality. From our experience, we have reached the conclusion that Carlos Castaneda explained the structure and functioning of the Energy Body in way that best suits or purposes. Most systems that work with such a concept as the Energy Body states that radiates beyond the physical body in the form of a sphere or egg however, Castaneda has presented an additional feature of the Energy Body that has never been explained. This feature is known as the Assemblage Point, which is the element of the Self that allows the individual to perceive the universe around them. The Assemblage Point is a point of extreme brilliance within the Energy Body and was discovered by sorcerers in antiquity. It is about the size of a tennis ball and is located just behind our right shoulder. If we imagine that everything that is perceivable by humans runs through the universe along its own "thread" of energy we would see that we share "reality" because the same threads run through everyone's Assemblage Point. In this way we can understand how people perceive the same things and in certain cases, perceive different things. For example, you are holding this and reading from a "book" printed upon "white paper" and letters are structured to formulate "words". This is because your Assemblage Point is in the same position mine is in, however, if it were in a different position altogether, we would not agree on these things. We may have a slight shift of the Assemblage Point that was unintentional and inborn that would not allow us to see the same colors. If our Assemblage Point is in the Position of someone whom is color blind, then they would not agree on what "color" the cover is.

The Habitual position of the Assemblage Point

As mentioned above, the Assemblage Point is located a short distanced off of the right shoulder blade. When it is in this Position we are able to share perceptions and agree with our fellow man. We have been taught to maintain this position of the Assemblage Point since we were children, our parents, teachers, etc. constantly explained to us what is "real" and what is not. Today, as adults, we continue to maintain this rigid mode of perception by talking to ourselves. Day and night our "internal dialogue" upholds the World. This internal chatter can, through disciplined practice, be silenced for extended periods of time and allow an individual to experience other perceptual realities. Although, we do not want to constantly be confined to the habitual position of the Assemblage Point, we must accept while going about our daily lives that it is necessary to maintain an agreement with our fellow humans.

Shifting and Moving the Assemblage Point

Now we are ready to consider the consequences of shifting and moving the Assemblage Point out of its habitual position. A Shift is the act of dislodging the Assemblage Point and allowing it to relocate to a new position within the Energy Body. A Movement of the Assemblage Point is the act of dislodging and moving it to a position beyond the Energy Body, stretching the Energy Body along with it as it goes. Obviously, shifts are far more common. A shift can be minor and not even noticed much (if at all) or it can be a severe shift that disrupts how we think and function. Minor shifts can occur from breaking patterns in our lives. An example would be a vegetarian who does not eat food containing beef, changing their diet abruptly. That person may feel stomach discomfort and other physical symptoms but it is still a minor shift with almost no noticeable psychological effect. Major shifts can occur for just as many reasons as the minor ones. Sever illness / injury, abnormal physical acts and dreaming are just a few examples of such larger shifts. For instance, if an individual ingests hallucinogenic mushrooms, they will experience things that others whom are maintaining the habitual position of the Assemblage Point will not agree upon. This person may "hear colors" or "see sounds", they may experience a whole world that others cannot. The mushrooms served to dislodge the Assemblage Point to the extent that will effect how they function for hours. Any text on Shamanic technique will give examples of how this is accomplished, from the use of mind altering plants to enduring physical pain.

The Order of the Voltec, too, has its own unique approaches to shifting the Assemblage Point. Moving the Assemblage Point is very different from a shift because it will allow one to experience perceptual modes that are not of the human condition. Movements rarely occur accidentally and are often the result of dedicated work within a particular system of the occult. A movement will change not only how you think and function, but it will change every aspect of your being and how you perceive the universe. The Order of the Voltec explains techniques for such Assemblage Point movements within the higher degrees.

The Voltec Tree of Night

A common graphic representation of potential Positions of the Assemblage Point takes form in the Cabalistic school. Commonly called the Tree of Life, this symbol is a map that shows positions of the Assemblage Point while pursuing the goals of the Right Hand Path. I will not go into detail about the Tree of Life proper, for there are 100s of texts that already serve that purpose. Those individuals that pursue the Left Hand Path, will eventually come across the "Reverse Side of the Tree of Life", which is explained within the works of Kenneth Grant among many other authors today. These individuals seek changes with the assistance of the Klippoth upon the Reverse Side of the Tree of Life. Traditionally, the Reverse Side is reached by ascending up the Tree of Life proper and crossing to the "Back", through Da'ath, and down the back eventually returning to Malkuth. Something that will stand out in the Voltec system is that we do not work upon the Tree of Life or the Reverse Side of the Tree of Life. Of course we do not limit ourselves by saying that we will never partake of such work on the conventional Tree of Life, however we have found that the changes we seek are actual positions of the Assemblage Point that are not located upon either the Tree of Life proper or the reverse Side of the Tree of Life. These positions vaguely resemble some of the qualities of the Reverse Side of the Tree of Life, however, we have repeatedly had experiences that have led us to comprehend an entirely different Tree. The graphic representation looks like the Tree of Life but inverted. After some conscious review of this strange occurrence, we have come to see how this alignment accurately represents what the Voltec Initiate attempts to accomplish. Its not about simply taking the Right Hand Path and flipping it over to show a polar opposite. It is about getting to the "Roots" of all experiences and potentiality that the other Trees grow from. Going up the front is not enough. Crossing to the Reverse Side is a start, however, it is still just the "other side" of what is already above the surface. To get to the essential aspects of the Self, to create a Godlike being that will ultimately gain perceptual freedom upon departure, one must dig below the surface. We, like the RHP, start at Malkuth but we descend down to Kether.

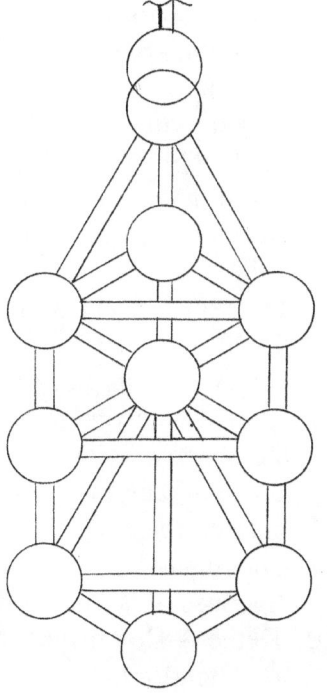

The diagram shows how the Dayside Malkuth overlaps with the Tree of Night, Malkuth. The overlapped area is called the "Wormwood Zone" and is the Point of Crossing into "Nod".

The Two Trees of Night

As the chapter on the structure of the Order of the Voltec will explain, the OV is divided into two separate, internal, groups. One for Stalkers and one for Dreamers. Each of these internal, "Houses" has its own Tree of Night showing the types of Sorcery that is approached within each of the Assemblage Point positions associated with each of the Power Zones and Tunnels. The work of the Order of the Voltec is largely based on the mastery of these 32 Positions of the Assemblage Point.

The Downward Path Tree of Night

The following is a list of the 32 Positions of the Stalker's Tree of Night and the type of Sorcery associated with each. Detailed explanations of the application of these types of Sorcery are the subject of the first two volumes in the "Downward Path into Nod" trilogy.

The Power Zones:
1) Malkuth—Sorcery of Departure (Onto the Tree of Night)
2) Yesod—Sorcery of Other Forms (Becoming the shadow Self in Nod)
3) Hod-Poison Sorcery (Killing the Dayside Influence)
4) Netzach-Energy Sorcery (Strengthening the Shadow Self)
5) Tipareth-Sorcery of the Voltec Agreement (Tempering the Shadow Self)
6) Geburah—Fire Sorcery (Refining the Shadow Self)
7) Chesed—Power Sorcery (Energy Deployment from the Shadow Self)
8) Binah—Faceless Sorcery (Making the Shadow Self Inaccessible)
9) Chokmah-Casting Thorns Sorcery (Removing All Avenues of Withdraw from Nod)
10) Kether—Downward Path Sorcery (Preparing for the 3rd Attention).

The Tunnels:
11) Amprodias - Sorcery of Detachment (Techniques of Detaching from the energy Traps of Occult thought and Practice).
12) Baratchial - Sorcery of Liberation (Techniques of Liberating stagnant energies within the Energy Body).
13) Gargophias - Sorcery of Egregores (Recognizing Egregores and not confusing them with other Sentient Beings, creating egregores, utilizing existing egregores, etc.).
14) Dagdagiel - Sorcery of Empathy (Consciousness Sharing between Voltec Sorcerers).
15) Hemethterith - Sorcery of Knowing Cycles (Receiving the Secrets of the Old Cycle Sorcerers and integrating them into the Voltec Current, understanding our hybrid of the Old and New Cycles).
16) Uriens - Sorcery of Silent Knowing (Arriving at Silent Knowing and differentiating Silent Knowing from other "received messages").
17) Zamradiel - Sorcery of Sexual Energy (Sexual Techniques of the Voltec Current and techniques of ecstasy).
18) Characith - Consuming Sorcery (The Art of Devouring, consuming energy from other sources, consuming physical material for energetic purposes, etc).
19) Temphioth - Sorcery of Male Energy (For Males, it is a total immersion in what they are Energetically and to learn to utilize their characteristics to their full potential; For females, it is a temporary abandonment of femininity and to assume a Male Energetic form when necessary).
20) Yamatu - Sorcery of the Flowery Dream (Legal Entheogens, Dream Entheogens for Stalkers, controlling the Entheogenic Perceptual Filters).
21) Kurgasiax - Sorcery of Atavisms (recovery of Atavisms and how to use them).
22) Lafcursiax - Lunar Sorcery of the Kalas (Dealing with Lunar Workings, obtainment and use of Kalas, and all new information concerning male secreted Kalas).

23) Malkunofat - Sorcery of Non-Time (Abandoning conventional time, recovery of memories of future, past and present memories).

24) Niantiel - Death / Rebirth Sorcery (Dealing with aspects of ones Death, Blood Sorcery, Death Energies, and the Dead, as well as Erasing Personal History and new Life as a Voltec Sorcerer).

25) Saksaksalim - Inversion Sorcery (RHP methods for LHP goals).

26) A'ano'nin - Sorcery of Distillation (Distilling consumable fluids, shifting from Gazing at the process, conscious selection of ingredients and proper procedure and use of distillates).

27) Parfaxitas - Sorcery of Blades (Sorcery involving shifts that are augmented by the preparation and use of swords and knives).

28) Tzuflifu - Sorcery of the Female Energy (For females, it is a total immersion into what they are and fortifying the Energy Body with its natural characteristics ; For males, it is a temporary abandonment of masculine energy and the ability to assume a Female Energy Body. The deployment of Female abilities are also covered).

29) Qulielfi - Sorcery of Traveling within the Shadow Self (Developing the Ability to Travel to any physical location within the Shadow Self and retain memories of the events, eventually leading to the physical manifestation of the Shadow Self).

30) Raflifu - Sorcery of the Unfiltered Self (Methods of Accessing the Shadow Self without interference from filters, working with Pure Expression of Will, etc).

31) Shalicu - Sorcery of Receiving from the Outside (Sorcery of Selective Accessibility, becoming Aware of Outside Influences and Transmissions of the Voltec Current).

32) Thantifaxath - Sound Sorcery (shifting via creating/producing sounds, receiving power songs and mantras in alternate states, and observing sounds).

The Outer Darkness Tree of Night

The Outer Darkness Tree of Night describes the associations of Dream Sorcery and its various positions of the Assemblage Point. This Tree serves as a map for the "House" in which the Dreamers of the Order of the Voltec operate (see "Internal Structure and the Degree System of the Order of the Voltec").

Dayside Malkuth: Ordinary Dreaming
Wormwood Zone: Dream Recall

Power Zones:
1) Malkuth—Ordinary Dreams of Significance
2) Yesod—Becoming Aware (Lucid Dreaming)
3) Hod-Waking from one dream into another
4) Netzach—Interdimensional Travel
5) Tipareth—Construction of the Dreaming Bed
6) Geburah—The Dreaming Body
7) Chesed—Dreaming Body Travel
8) Binah—The Double
9) Chokmah—Teleportation
10) Kether—The Fire From Within

The Tunnels:
11) Amprodias—Dreams of Death
12) Baratchial—House of Allies
13) Gargophias—Voltec Current
14) Dagdagiel—Encountering the Human Mold
15) Hemthterith—Place of Songs
16) Uriens—Lucid Sexual Dreams
17) Zamradiel—Dreaming with Others (Sorcerer's Gathering)
18) Characith—Shapeshifting Dreams
19) Temphioth—Dreaming Emmisary
20) Yamatu—Dream Invasions
21) Kurgasiax—Dream Feeding
22) Lafcursiax—House of Deities

23) Malkunofat—House of Scouts
24) Niantiel—House of Egregores
25) Saksaksalim—Dream Tomes
26) A'ano'nin—Dream Artifacts
27) Parfaxitas—Dream Smoke (Calea Zacatechichi, Sal via Divinorum and Wormwood)
28) Tzuflifu—Prophetic Lucid Dreams
29) Qulielfi—False Lucidity
30) Raflifu—Lucid Dreams of Times Past
31) Shalicu—Mastering Physical Sleeping Positions
32) Thantifaxath—The Dream Diary

This list helps illustrate how maintaining these Positions of the Assemblage Point by either physical "Stalking" techniques or by "Dreaming" is associated with the map of the Tree of Night. The practices, goals and effects associated with each Position are just a sample of the possibilities that become available to the Voltec Initiate. Detailed techniques are shared within the Order of the Voltec.

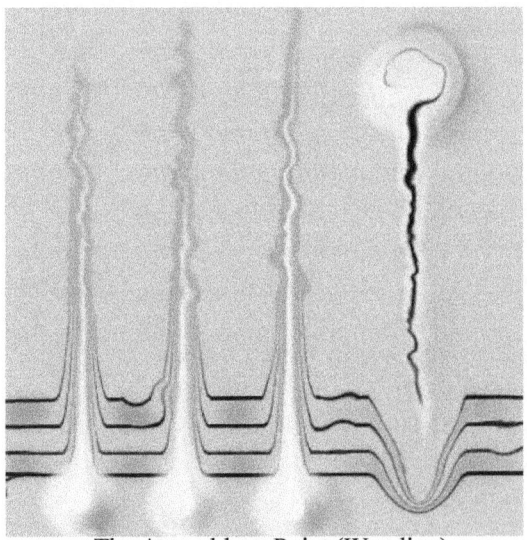

The Assemblage Point (Wendigo)

Theory and Practice within the Order of the Voltec

The fundamental premise of the Order of the Voltec is that of sorcery in any form; That there is immense power right before us all the time, and that we have the capability to tap into that power at will. There are worlds upon worlds for us to delve into and explore, we simply need to become capable of entering into those worlds. A Voltec is concerned with abstract practicalities, and what I mean by this is we are geared towards action that is propelled by abstract thought. Sitting around reading all day will not give you power or help you become a shape shifter. Our practices have shown actual results. We do not pursue that which does not help us achieve our immediate goals.

The Voltec starts with a basic set of premises that concern the very nature of the universe in which we operate. First, we regard perception as the root of subjective existence. Time is understood by us as the perceivable by-product of attention, and thus the quality of a living organism's attention determines how they will experience the flow of time. The Voltec seeks to be continuously aware that there are two fields of perception within our immediate grasp. There are configurations of energy which we transform into physical data through our five senses, and there is, on top of that a social description which we have been taught to impose upon those things we have learned to perceive. This social aspect of perception is, as I have said, an inheritance. It is passed down to us by our ancestors, and it is modified according to the needs of these people at particular periods in time. Without this social description, the world would lack meaning. All of our ideas about the world and the way that it works have been conditioned by the tenets of our social description. Our most inner ideas and beliefs have grown out of this ancestral heirloom, and we are taught, out of our instinctual avoidance of the unknown, to avoid questioning it.

We know so little about some of the most important things that we encounter on a daily basis but, because we have accepted a set of common social explanations for these things, we never really bother to examine them and acknowledge their immensely mysterious nature. Take death for instance. We think about death in a certain way and treat it as something with which we have an abundance of experience. What do we really know about death? We think it is the end of life because we see that when a living being dies, they resign all signs of life and their body begins to disappear. That is all we know, because that is all we see. Everything else that we think we know about death is a result of the influence of our socialization. Death is dark. Death is the end. Death is cold. Death is bad. These are all ideas that have come into existence by using values that are socially construed. We have been taught to place a value on everything, and this social system of values plays a tremendous role in limiting our capability of assessing the universe in terms that are more in line with energetic truth.

The social aspect of perception tells us what we are, what is important in the world and what we should not bother paying attention to. We are divorced from nature because we disregard anything that does not have social value. That which has social value is immediately gratifying to the greatest of all social fictions, our very selves. The first and primary task of the Voltec sorcerer is to recognize the social description of the world for what it is, and systematically begin separating this description from what they actually perceive. This is no easy task, as our socialization is the only tool we have for interacting with the world around us. This being acknowledged, we do not want to throw away our ability to interact, but we do wish to have the capability of isolating the social aspect of something and then relating to it in more sophisticated ways. Lets take death again for instance. We can examine everything that we have been taught about death, and then separate everything that is social from that which is actually perceivable. If we are able to do this, then we might get closer to the essence of what death really is and perhaps even get a glimpse into its mysterious nature. This will never happen if we only regard it in set terms that have been unexamined and handed down to us as a convenient way to comfort ourselves in a strange and mysterious universe.

When we are capable of separating the social part of perception, we will also become capable of beginning the formation of our own field of reality, or what we could call a second version of the world. Voltec sorcerers come together to help each other reach what Castaneda might call a non-ordinary consensus. The world is made up of cultural and social agreements. Our realities are a consequence of what we emphasize in our thoughts. The Nightside of the Voltec is also made up of consensual agreements. Ones that are vastly different from what the average person is accustomed to. The Nightside, or land of Nod, in which we operate is a result of the redeployment of our energy and the result of emphasizing that which had previously gone unnoticed. Nod is the Nightside of the Tree of Life, the Unknown, the Shadow Realm, or the Nagual of the Toltecs. The Voltec, realizing the conditional nature of reality, willfully isolates themselves from the perceptual and consensual agreements of the average human being. New agreements are made, and new ideas are emphasized. In this way a second field of awareness can be cultivated and strengthened.

A central theme in Toltec sorcery and many other shamanic traditions is the role that our internal self talk, or internal dialogue plays in shaping our perception. Ken Eagle Feather, a well known new age writer says that *" Don Juan (Castaneda's sorcery teacher) refers to the combined elements of a world view as an "inventory." He says that an inventory makes us invulnerable, which is why we go about making them in the first place (Fire, 85-86). It makes us invulnerable because it acts as a set of filters and mirrors, determining what enters consciousness. When Don Juan brought inorganic beings into a house, for example, Castaneda couldn't perceive them. They were part of a Toltec inventory Castaneda had not yet learned. Since his inventory didn't contain that element, he could not purposefully align his energy with them. Therefore, he couldn't perceive them. As a result, he was protected from their influence"* (Eagle Feather, 1995). Human beings talk to themselves constantly. This is how we define and refine our daily world. Our personal inventory is made up of the social agreements that we have made with our society and our internal dialogue, or what we incessantly tell ourselves about everything. We inherit our internal dialogue from our ancestors as a part of their description of the world. As we slowly dismantle and restructure this dialogue, we seek to replace its items with new ideas. Ideas which are based more around our goals as black magicians. The process of becoming a Voltec is intimately connected with our relearning how to think. It is a task of replacing the old items of our mental inventory with entirely new one. This new description of the world is where the Voltec sorcerer resides, away from the concerns of the everyday person, and isolated from energies that will wear us down prematurely.

Our lives are a result of what we have been taught to emphasize. As Voltecs, we choose to emphasize that which is normally feared or discarded altogether. We emphasize and immerse ourselves in the darkness in order to discover its silent secrets. We emphasize the fundamental energetic nature of our physical bodies and the power that our minds have to shape them according to our will. We emphasize the indisputable fact that our dreams are the gateway to immense power, and that by learning to consciously interact while in dreaming, we can begin to acquaint ourselves with our double nature. For the Voltec sorcerer, belief is indeed a means to and end, not an end in itself. This is one of the basic premises of chaos magic, and one that we agree with completely. The only difference may be in our understanding and application of the power of belief to actually alter the very core nature of what we are. For the Voltec, the Left Hand Path leads farther and farther away from what is known to be human. Taking this path costs infinitely more than one might imagine, yet if it is traversed with a mix of confidence and respect it will yield delights undreamed of.

In order to begin and sustain the transformation from interested occult student to Voltec sorcerer, we have to take real life, concrete and practical measures. Surrounding ourselves with the trappings of magic will not be enough to cause true change in accordance with our well refined will.

Dark symbolism and the embodiment of seemingly 'evil ' characteristics typify the modern practitioner of LHP magic. The display of these qualities is usually based on the need to feel special, powerful and superior to the average person. The black magician of the traditional modern LHP believes themselves to be accessing a wellspring of actual dark energy (typically this is via the intervention of the Prince of Darkness in one form or another.) At first the self-proclaimed black magician is accessing new energy, the same way that a teenage boy will when he goes to his first nudy bar with his comrades. There will be new sights and sounds, new feelings about self and world, yet in the end the only way to get back to that energy is to go back to the source of the original experience. This the black magician does again and again, but instead of using the newly liberated energy to free their perceptual entrainment, they push it back into re-enforcing their LHP world view. This creates a closed circuit, and even though the black magician may have an expanded world view, it is still just a view and as such extremely limiting. It may also be a hazardous world view, if the root motivation for performing black magic and being LHP is fear based because the liberated energy is actually feeding an inflated ego and a huge amount of self-importance. This can only end in death, not the immortality of one's isolate psyche centric existence, and is in no way different than the pursuits of ordinary people with their daily rituals and self absorption.

The modern black magician is in many ways worse off than the average person because they use their magical accomplishments to feed an elitist viewpoint, while they believe that they are fortifying their psyche. There is no magic in this, as many an elitist organization and school of thought has easily swayed weak, yet imaginative minds to serve their self-deification. Unfortunately most LHP and other magical organizations are really nothing more than semi-intricate congregations of hero worshipers, who don't have the desire to change at a truly profound level.

Any type of personal rebellion against religion, society or the self will definitely liberate new and unused energy, however the ego will almost always cling to this expanded consciousness as a new possession and as a truth or even 'the truth,' but this new consciousness becomes as mundane as the mundane world once was, and new stimuli must be sought out.

I have made a simple chart that applies to the traditional modern LHP practitioner.

THE BLACK MAGICIAN
(fear based personal motives)
+
+

BLACK MAGIC
(either uses LHP magic and philosophies to have power over others or to liberate energy and have new LHP experiences.)
+
+
+

EXPANDED AWARENESS
(Used to reinforce original personal motives and to reinforce current LHP belief system.)

The Voltec is the modern sorcerer, and Adept of the LHP, and ultimately seeks freedom from this illusory cycle. With the late Anton Szandor LaVey, the LHP became forever associated with Satanism and the image of a Prince of Darkness, but before the Church Of Satan, I can bet you that virtually no one had heard of the LHP. The ToS took it quite a step further and the LHP became the vehicle for an intellectual and black magical elite, but the traditional context that the term LHP actually has is, at its root, Shamanic. To the sorcerer and shaman, the LHP is the one taken by those brave (or crazy) individuals that leads away from a limited and fixed world view in favor of a much larger universe of many truths and possibilities. The LHP leads us to the Left Side of Awareness. We also call this the Nightside due to our initiatory background, and to the terms applicability. The Left Side or Nightside of Awareness is everything that you do not perceive right now, and cannot perceive under normal conditions. These conditions can be perceived and experienced through non-ordinary means. The vow of the Voltec is to never come to depend on specific non-ordinary practices to achieve freedom of perception. A practice must always be recognized as only a platform from which the vaulter may hurl them into the night, experiencing that which they may, but coveting nothing, lest they be weighed down and encumbered at their next leap.

Starting their journey on the Tree of Night, the Voltec conceives of the Power Zones and Tunnels of Set as a three dimensional extension of the Right Hand Path Tree of Life starting at Malkuth. The Tree of Night is not a reflection of the Tree of Life, but another conceptual alternative altogether. For the adept of the Left Hand Path, the Tree of Life ceases to exists as soon as they begin their decent into the Tunnels. The Left Hand Path initiation has nothing to do with the process as conceived by Crowley.

It begins in Malkuth, and the entrance to the Tunnels are not accessible in the way that the Paths of the Tree are. This means that a Left Hand Path paradigm is the key to opening the perceptual doors that lead to the Tunnels to begin with. Just as the Path of Dreaming is the river that runs into the abyss of the Nagual, so the Tunnels of Set are tributaries leading into that river. These are specific points of emphasis that the sorcerer uses to orient themselves as they purposely fade into the shadows, while retaining and strengthening their individual awareness. This is in direct opposition to the process of initiation on the Tree of Life proper, as the Right Hand Path initiate strives to categorize and classify to the point of obsession in order to make everything fit onto the Tree.

The Left Hand Path Adept does not have any relation to the Tree of Life. If they did, it would imply that they had started their initiation on the Right Hand Path. For us, we never went that way, or if we did, we turned around at a given point. The Crowley, or Right Hand Path conception of the Tree of Life insists that the black brother is created when they fail to cross the abyss successfully. This is the only point of view they could possibly have after their subjective initiation in that system. This paradigm implies that the imperfections of the individual magician will cause them a cosmic punishment if they fail. Fail in what? Crowley is somewhat vague in this area. He also implies that there is nothing the Adeptus can do to ensure a successful crossing. This reeks of Judeo-Catholic predestination, and is abhorrent from a LHP perspective.

The LHP is the path of those who diverge from the main stream of modern human consciousness in order to access their greater perceptual capabilities. Any divergent action by the individual from a right side, main stream point of view is extremely threatening to the continuity of the whole, and thus dubbed with a quality called 'evil.' This is why people who have a drive to be different than the norm will often try to personify a powerful opposing force, such as the Prince of Darkness. At least with Satan, there is the cool imagery and the promise of power, not to mention a great excuse to feel more important than everything around you. To the Voltec, this is nothing more than a form of insanity, not unlike many others. The true LHP sorcerer has lost all desire to oppose their fellow human, and deals with them in very special terms leaving themselves thus free to begin the restructuring of themselves.

Anonymity and Our Consensus

The creation of our Second Field or Night Side begins with the understanding that such an avenue of activity and existence can be molded to suit our desire and purposes. We begin with the expansion of ideas and the formation of agreements, or new perceptual contracts made with one another as sorcerers and fellow Voltecs. A critical examination of our native socialization is crucial in being able to truly assess our effectiveness in solidifying such contracts. The next step is practical action. We begin to act upon these new fundamental ideas, thus generating the energetic movement of thought in a specific direction. Our thoughts and actions combine with the thoughts and actions of each other, and so an entire socio-perceptual consensus is brought into being.

It begins by simply challenging the known constraints of our culture and selectively putting forth an effort to countermand the energy that we have already put into motion by accepting our role in this culture. We take one major aspect of how most human beings, including ourselves currently living in the western world, and we choose to challenge that way with other behaviors that are diametrically opposed. Most human beings live and thrive during the hours of daylight. The sorcerer of the Left Hand Path has always reigned supreme over the night and the advantages to living in such a nocturnal fashion are many. Of course, I do not expect that everyone will be able to strictly adhere to a totally nocturnal schedule. This would be ridiculous, especially for those of us with families and children. However, I have had the opportunity to live in this manner for many years and I must highlight the desirability of such an arrangement. First, living at night allows us to separate ourselves from the heavy and imposing thoughts of others. This is extremely important if we are to consider the power that other people's thoughts have to influence our own. So few people are active between the sensitive hours of midnight till about four thirty, or five in the morning. This time is ideal for ritual work, and the residual effects of being out of sight from the masses can be felt on several levels, including the physical. Not having to expose ourselves to the rays of the sun helps tremendously in keeping our youthful appearance, and there are so many 24 hour stores and facilities that dealing with crowds is a nonexistent problem. Being active while the rest of the world sleeps adds significant power to our ability in creating a second field of reality. This field becomes as real as our primary field when the momentum of our thoughts and actions has reached a peak. If you find it impossible to work and live exclusively at night, try at least to arrange for periods of time when you can reasonably do so.

For instance, at my place of work there is the occasional opportunity to rotate shifts and I can work at night for months at a time before rotating back to other hours. Even these shorter immersions into the darkness will help the Sorcerer rid themselves of the calcified, stagnant energy that they have accumulated over time. Living primarily during the hours of night helps acquaint us with the darkness as a tangible, malleable and potent source of power that we can learn to interact with intimately. Many of our Voltec ritual workings and meditations are directed at helping us develop a relationship with the darkness, as well as practical exercises for using shadow as a portal into other realms. We learn to cast shadow around us that we may fortify, protect and nurture the Nightside of our Awareness. Using those elements that go unnoticed, we create a hidden doorway out of the world of daily affairs.

Utilizing the inventory of a sorcerer, we seek to emphasize dreams as a field of great importance. The Toltecs discovered that dreaming was an area of infinite possibility, and they treated their dreams as if they were real events. This is what I mean by emphasis. Events that simply took place at a different level of Awareness. Dream sorcery is one of the foundational concerns of the Voltec. Beginning with the command to find a specific item (Castaneda used his hands, and so did I) while in a dream, the sorcerer develops the capability of becoming fully aware while dreaming. We also become capable of becoming aware that we are falling asleep. Learning to dream awake, or have lucid dreams is a skill that takes years to develop. With the development of dreaming comes the emergence of the dreaming body, the energy body, or the other. The other, carefully molded to perfection is a direct expression of our dual nature. This double becomes an active extension of the sorcerer themselves, until there is no difference between the Voltec and the double itself. Surrounding ourselves with an environment that is non ordinary in itself is also a powerful step in creating our Nightside. I grew up in white, middle class, suburban America. Something within me naturally rejected many things about this world, and when I finally went out into the world on my own, I began to experiment with living environments that I found more stimulating. I rented apartments and painted them black, red and purple. I fashioned huge Satanic alters and played with different kinds if lighting. Over the years I learned to shape my immediate living environment in ways that helped me sustain altered perception and strengthen the development of my Nightside.

There are a million ways that one can fashion their environment in order to enhance their sorcery goals. One can keep it simple or pour as much complexity into it as one desires, as long as the end result helps you feel as though you are living in a dimension altogether different than that of the every day world. While we are in our fortress of shadows, we will be isolated from the pull of the Dayside. This place is a physical point in time and space that will enable us to slow down time, emphasize our sorcery objectives and keep the energy that we store protected from unnecessary dispersion. A self made environment needs certain essential conditions for it to function at its best. First, communication with the outside world must be able to be shut off at will. Phones can be turned off or kept in drawers until needed. Windows may be covered over with aluminum foil to achieve continuous night and to help eradicate our day to day routines.

The ancient Toltecs viewed and understood the world in terms that are much different that the ones we westerners are accustomed to. As Voltec sorcerers, we have taken some of the basic premises of the Toltecs and adopted them to our knowledge of the evolution of the Left Hand Path. The Toltecs began their exploration into sorcery with the fundamental assertion that we live in a universe, or multiverse of energy. Modern human beings assert that the universe is a material, concrete realm made up of solid objects. This is of course true, but the Toltec, and, subsequently, the Voltec understand that the world is essentially composed of energy. This energy moves at different rates and the end result is what we perceive as a world of solidity. Unfortunately, the way our senses have been shaped to perceive the world dictates that we interpret our experiences in terms of the physical and solid. The underlying energetic nature of the world goes unacknowledged because it does not appear to have any relevance to our lives, or survival as humans.

This energetic paradigm is how the Voltec sorcerer approaches reality. It is not a matter of belief that motivates us to adopt this fundamental basis, but our actual experiences in dealing with the world according to energetic terms. Power is accumulated, not by how much one believes in something, but by the knowledge and understanding that is earned when one experiences the non ordinary and higher states of Awareness. We deal with the universe in terms of perception and energy. The Toltec understood that, as beings composed of energy, we could interact with the world in terms of energy. This is an idea that is in almost total opposition to western values. The average human being deals with the world in terms of social and material worth. Energy is something that causes the lights to go on, not the underlying structure of everything we are and can become. In the modern western paradigm, one's potential is also based on social and material expectations.

The Voltec starts with the basic premise that the concrete world is the result of an energetic reality which lies just beneath the surface. The Voltec sorcerer deals in terms of energy, rather that in terms of the material or social. This means that for us, the emphasis is on identifying, accumulating and storing energy. This energy is then used to fuel our sorcery pursuits and to strengthen our own counter-consensus. We, like the ancient Toltecs, have come to understand that each person is born with a determined amount of energy, which we then employ in our socially determined pursuits. Chief among these activities is forming and maintaining a sense of who we are as individuals. Our self image, and its constant maintenance continuously saps the majority of the personal energy that we have at our disposal. The formation of our Voltec counter-consensus demands that we learn how to free our energy, which we have been forced to employ in ways that have been determined completely by the social constraints of our modern culture. Like the vampire, the Voltec sorcerer eventually casts no image in a mirror, as they redefine and re-experience the boundaries of the self.

We enter the Nightside by first calling attention to the existence of certain features of that dimension, and then by a process of selective reinforcement. By agreeing on the existence of the energy double, and by slowly experiencing the effects of this phenomenon, we reinforce its objective existence. When enough sorcerers experience the double, we begin to create a cognitive inventory concerning its attributes. Our combined energy is directed towards the creation of the double, and it is thus born into existence. This is the process of reemphasis that I am talking about. The consensus that the Voltec creates with one another becomes a self sustaining field of activity. The nourishment of such a field is directly connected to our anonymity as creatures of the night. In our case, secrets do beget power. The less others know of our Nightside, the easier it is for us to keep it safely insulated from the destructive influence of the common culture.

When we learn to handle the world in terms of sorcery, we place value on things that go unnoticed for most. We value our freedom. Actual freedom is the freedom to evolve beyond the watered down expectations of our current culture. We value time. It is time that we regard as an irreplaceable resource within which to change ourselves according to our collective will. We emphasize magic as an ever present force that saturates every atom of our bodies, a force that is at our continual disposal. Our task is to free ourselves from the trappings of our native social order, as this has always been one of the major goals of those who have tread the Left Hand Path. Our anonymity is that of beings who dwell half in shadow. Our consensus is the weight of our collective perceptual entrainment, carefully and willfully constructed around the foundational understandings of generations of sorcerers.

The Eternal Black Flame

In the true spirit of the predator, we Voltecs have taken that which we desire and have discarded that which no longer applies. That which we desire is that which works for us, that which strengthens us and that which is in our best interest at all times. These priorities have developed directly from the precepts of the Church of Satan and its basic philosophies. While we retain the seeds of the word of Indulgence within each of us, we must also acknowledge the essential changes that have occurred over time. These changes are a part of our evolution as those who have chosen the path of the outsider. There are those who have resisted such natural and unnatural transformations, yet this is usually a symptom of unrefined nostalgia, combined with a need to define the Self in terms that cause a sense inflated importance. The Voltec has come to understand that inflated importance is not the same as self deification, and it is the antithesis of the true principles of immortality. I have met many adepts and magicians over the years claiming an affinity with black magic and the Left Hand Path, but there have been so few who have grown beyond their own human need and compulsion to feel powerful in the face of a world filled to the brim with real challenges. Many of the would be sorcerers that I have encountered simply chose the dark path as a very real way to avoid the demands of this world. Their sense of inadequacy drove them into the shadows, and there they cowered with others who had all learned the fine art of reinforcing their own contrived, bombastic elitism.

The fascinating thing about this common misapplication of Left Hand Path philosophy, is that if it is understood in more sophisticated terms, the true spirit of the antinomian way can be seen. That original impulse that causes us to reject the mediocre ideals of the common person, is the spark that creates the first stirring of the Black Flame within. What begins as a desire to separate one's self from the trappings of societal expectations, eventually leads to a desire to affiliate with others of like mind. The Black Flame must be carefully nurtured very early on to avoid the development of an unjustified and false sense of grandeur. An individual does not become one of the elite by simply embracing what they believe to be the marks of superiority. They do not become more than human by mere affiliation with an organization that caters to their actual weaknesses and then promotes them based off of a cycle of mutual magical mental masturbation.

What is this elitism that the Church of Satan has always claimed to have special understanding of? With this question comes a myriad of other questions concerning the nature of what we, as creative beings should consider being the desirable qualities of a superior or elite people. Most would agree that good health and physical prowess should be among the more fundamental of these qualities. Few would dare to argue this point, but how many sorcerers and their like have you met that are at their own peak of health and living a physically active lifestyle? Many times, it seems that the pursuit of the black arts lends itself to the rationale that one may justifiably ignore such mundane issues. The reality of the situation is that these types of basic issues are also the most important. Here is where I must agree with the Anton LaVey and the CoS. An out of shape, pasty, mid level office worker of above average intelligence, with no ambition to strive for any type of personal or professional excellence, has very little to offer the collective energy of the Left Hand Path. Now, take this same type of individual and inject them with a wholly unreasonable sense of importance and an interest in the occult. The end result here is most often what we encounter as the priests and high priests of the dark traditions. These are people whose egos are so frail, that they are drawn to promises of power without the weight of any kind of responsibility for what they do. If you are desperate and clever enough, you too can eventually become a priestess or priest in any number of organizations supposedly dedicated to the Prince of Darkness.

This line of thought brings me directly to a few of the most important contributions made by the original Black Pope, Anton Szandor LaVey. The Satanic Bible, first published in 1969, is a living and historical testimony to the economic, social and spiritual state of the human race of the western world during that time. That book encapsulated the essence of the reality of the undercurrent that ran through American society from the roaring 20s all the way until this present moment. That energetic undercurrent was, and is alive. Its name is Satan, and its word is Indulgence. LaVey did not simply recognize the true carnal nature of humanity he perpetually lived in a reality where the shadows existed in the foreground of his perception. In an age when human interaction was dependent on the use of superficial social niceties, Anton LaVey became a spokesperson for the grainy, dark and truthful world that coexists with that of the every day. The Satanic outlook on life, espoused upon in The Satanic Bible naturally creates the conditions whereby certain questions must be answered. As the questions arose, so the American father of Satanic thought carefully considered, and answered them in turn. The apparent result of this is known as the Nine Satanic Statements, the Eleven Satanic Rules of the Earth and the Nine Satanic Sins. These basic written statements become actual guidelines for the Satanist and adherent of the Left Hand Path. They are more than just suggestions for behavior; they are ways of viewing and relating to reality that, for the most part, cause a continued shift in perception for the black magician. The nature of this alteration is based on the fact that the satanic stance is constructed to oppose the established social norm.

The Eleven Satanic Rules of the Earth are incredibly akin to the stalking principles of the Toltec sorcerer, in that they prescribe special behaviors geared towards helping the sorcerer achieve the best results in any given situation. Rule Number one states *"Do not give opinions or advice unless you are asked"* (LaVey, 1967). This rule plays off of the all too human tendency to disregard anything that does not involve the self. LaVey understood that people's concerns basically revolved around their own lives, worries and passions. He studied human interactions and then applied his findings in order to achieve observable results. This Satanic rule resonates perfectly with the Voltec's understanding of the importance of conserving personal power. Why waste your energy giving advice and opinions to beings who aren't actually asking this of you? Let's face it, most of the time, when people are complaining, they don't want or expect any real substantial feedback from us. Dale Carnegie give us extremely valuable insight, that applies directly to this principle in his book *How to Win Friends and Influence People*. Carnegie illustrates several effective methods to use that will *"make people Like you,"* (112) my top favorites being *"be a good listener. Encourage others to talk about themselves,"* *"talk in terms of the other person's interests,"* and *"make the other person feel important-and do it sincerely"* (112). This is lesser black magic at its best, and certainly worth adding to the Voltec sorcerer's personal arsenal. LaVey's rule number two, *"Do not tell your troubles to others unless you are sure they want to hear them,"* is a perfect follow up with rule number one, and another gem of black magical psychology. Rule number eight states, *"do not complain about anything to which you need not subject yourself."* This Satanic Rule of the Earth mirrors the principles of Voltec warriorship, as derived from the writing of Carlos Castaneda. Human beings waste enormous amounts of precious energy reflecting and complaining about conditions that they have either created themselves, or simply need not subject themselves to. Living with this state of mind implies senility. We are the architects of our lives, and the sorcerer has taken an oath to push this realization to its most unnatural limits. Complaining about one's predicaments, while taking no action to change them is tantamount to self imposed slavery. This is the ultimate expression of accepting no responsibility for one's life or actions. Needless to say, this is the typical modus operandi of the Right Hand Path adherent. It is the mentality of the herd, and is absolutely vile from our perspective. The sorcerer of the Left Hand Path can strongly sense this mentality in others, almost as if it were a poisonous stench that only they can smell.

The Nine Satanic Statements make their appearance on page 25, of the Avon edition of the Satanic Bible, just before the Book of Satan. This Satanic set of philosophical points of departure form what many would consider to be the basic beliefs of LaVeyan Satanism. Statement number one reads, *"Satan represents indulgence, instead of abstinence!"* This exclamation automatically sets up the perfect conditions for a most devious trap. The Left Hand Path initiate, who fails to understand the nature and virtue of true, balanced indulgence, will inevitably fall prey to one of many potential pitfalls. When The Satanic Bible was first published, this statement alone became one of the most misinterpreted parts of the newly emerging satanic movement. Because of the inherently rebellious nature of those individuals who chose to embrace this long awaited socio-spiritual rebellion, the indulgence of Satanism became a most convenient excuse to engage one's senses and carnal desires to the point of self destruction. This was also very true of Aleister Crowley's catch phrase, *"Do What Thou Wilt Shall be the Whole of the Law."* As we all know, self destruction is tantamount to sin for the adept of the Left Hand Path, and thus seen as something that no awakened individual would consider involving themselves in. The theme of Satanic indulgence, and its related ideas are alive and well for both the Modern Satanist and the Voltec sorcerer.

The theme of indulgence as an almost Aeonic word is the natural consequence of the evolutionary need to reject abstinence and asceticism as the only viable paths to attainment. Denial of the self, particularly the carnal self will, for most result in only delusions of spiritual grandeur and inflated self importance. The tendency when engaging in magical and mystical practices that have self denial as their main components is for the individual to believe that they are doing some thing that is "better" and more spiritual than their fellow beings. They elevate themselves to the exalted position of Adeptus Expemptus, and continue to engage in beliefs and behaviors that will only reinforce the illusion of divinity that they have worked so hard to create. The truly spiritual religions, most of which are shamanic, have always retained the idea that spiritual value is not something that can be determined or measured by the standards of humankind. For the true sorcerer, the smell and texture of the dirt beneath their feet is just as pure and holy as the most expensive frankincense, burning in a censer of pure gold.

The indulgence of the common person is the indulgence of the adept of the Right Hand Path. It is engaged in without thought, and used to fortify an ego that cannot understand or recognize real strength. The indulgence of the true black magician is a purposeful interaction, done with a refined intent that has the momentum of sheer will behind it. The rest of the Nine Satanic Statements are just as applicable for us today as they were for the Satanists of the 60s and 70s. The emphasis and application of these declarations may have evolved, but overall they are an important basis for the adept of the Left Hand Path from any school.

What I consider to be the crowning glory of these satanic insights and guidelines is called the Nine Satanic Sins (LaVey, 1987). Here are nine manifestations of modern human thought and behavior that should be understood by every Satanist, or black magician. These are human weaknesses that LaVey wanted us to take an active part in opposing on a regular basis. My favorites include Satanic Sin number one, Stupidity, which refers to the kind of stupidity engendered by the mass acceptance of herd mentality and the unfortunate consequences of such abundant ignorance; Satanic Sin number two, Pretentiousness, which has become an epidemic in our society, primarily due to the continuing trend of lowering our human standards of excellence, and Satanic Sin number eight, Counterproductive Pride. This is the primary affliction of mankind, and the seed of our potential demise. Counterproductive pride abounds in every human circle and endeavor. This is intimately connected to the illusion that we are immortal beings whose affairs are of the utmost importance in the grand scheme of things.

Pentagonal Revisionism: A Five Point Program (LaVey, 1988) *"reflects attitudes which allow others to decide whether they wish to align themselves with Satanism or not."* LaVey Explains, *"Each is necessary for Satanic change to take place. When asked what we're 'doing', here's the answer."* This five point program begins with an explanation of what LaVey refers to as stratification, the fundamental *"point on which all the others ultimately rest."* This concept is the acknowledgement that human beings belong to a diverse spectrum of talents, potentials and innate strengths. The principle of stratification rests primarily on the belief that people are not really created equal, and that even if they are, somewhere along the line most of them succumb to the well established modern path of mediocrity. The Voltec sorcerer does in fact embrace the idea of a natural stratification and we clearly see that western society has, for the most part, become a place where the weak can thrive happily at the expense of the strong. Stratification is the ideal social result of any Left Hand Path philosophy applied to the outward world, however, the ultimate goals of the sorcerer who enters our conclave of shadows has little to do with our fellow women and men. As black magicians, we do often clearly see the way things should work, but it is the full time job of the revolutionary or the fool to make social change their personal business. The Voltec stands outside time, as we know it, and the ultimate destiny of humankind holds less and less interest for us as we move further away from the concerns and obsessions of the average person.

The fifth point of the program calls for *"the opportunity for anyone to live within a total environment of his or her choice, with mandatory adherence to the aesthetic and behavioral standards of same."* This point, in particular is of great interest to the Order of the Voltec. A good portion of our sorcery training is directed at the creation, establishment and sustaining of our own personal Nightside. This is our own hatch into the unknown, and whether he knew it or not, LaVey was hinting at an extremely important principle in applied sorcery. In order to recondition our own personal energetic flow, a flow which is set into motion by our thoughts and is responsible for every facet of our lives, we must pull away from the heavy influence of the energetic consensus of our fellow beings. The creation of total environments would be an ideal way to aid in this reconditioning. We become what we think, and what we think is determined by what we have accepted in reference to the prevailing social order of the time.

Every Voltec sorcerer will be called to put forth their best effort at creating their own total environment. These are the basic magickal principles which allow the ritual chamber to work in that way that it is supposed to, but magnified to an extent that one's very essence and physical self will change as a result of their chosen environmental influences. We are first changing what we see and interact with on a daily basis. This causes a natural modification in our internal dialogue, which in turn continues to influence every other aspect of our being.

Since total environments have yet to become manifest in our present time, it is up to the ingenuity of the sorcerer to design, create, sustain and modify their own personal sphere of influence. I, myself practiced these steps for many years. In my own experience, simply living a nocturnal lifestyle automatically sets up the necessary preconditions for freeing one's self from the influence of the daily world. Living almost completely at night is not such a far fetched affair as it might have been a few decades ago. There are plenty of career choices and vocations that actually encourage this lifestyle, but even if this schedule is impossible, much can be done to begin orchestrating dramatic environmental changes in one's life.

Let us, for a moment turn our attention to the concept of "the elite" in a Left Hand Path context. Every black magician and Satanist has a different view on this topic, no matter how slight. The official Church of Satan website offers an abundance of information on the Church of Satan's outlook on why they consider themselves to be "elite," or an "alien elite" and the Temple of Set has accumulated volumes of material that also attest to this claim. Just as with anything else in the Voltec system of sorcery, the qualifying criteria for being elite stems from energetic truths perceivable to other sorcerers. Can the Voltec move their Assemblage Point? Do they have a masterful degree of control over themselves and their lives? Much like modern days Satanists, Voltecs are "non-joiners". We do not need an organization to validate our magic or our selves. The Order of the Voltec exists as a means of transmitting, storing and utilizing ancient knowledge that has made itself highly applicable in a modern shamanistic context. This is one of the key reasons that our members remain totally anonymous from one another until they have reached the third degree and are ready to assume the duties of the fourth.

The Not-Doing of Shadow
(Treating ordinary reality in non-ordinary ways)

The Voltec's immersion into Nod begins with the basic acknowledgement that our world is held together by our every day actions and thoughts. These ordinary endeavors can be thought of as the doing of the average person. Our doing in thought and action keeps the Assemblage Point, and thus our perception stable and uniform. It is the sorcerer who seeks to uproot the Assemblage Point from its customary position, and this is done by treating the most predominant features of our every day worlds in the most non-ordinary of ways. To begin with, each sorcerer becomes slowly capable of acting within two separate and distinct paradigms. The first is the paradigm of the average person, where life and death are set, predictable events, old age is an inevitable decline in physical strength and prowess, and sex is an all powerful driving force. These are just a few of the normal, every day chunks of cognition that the average person takes for granted, and the path of the average individual has an eventual end that is just as average. All our regular energy is normally employed in keeping the boundaries of our world intact. This is an extremely consuming affair, and those individuals who stray from the safety of the herd are considered outcast. There are very good reasons for this.

The Sorcerer knowingly decides to treat ordinary reality in non-ordinary ways, and the effect that this has is a gradual movement of the Assemblage Point, as well as the expansion of the sorcerer's subjective/objective Nightside. Let's take the realm of sex for example since it is such a consuming area, energetically speaking. We seem to most often find ourselves as being subjected to our sexual desires, as slaves are subject to the whims of their masters. We let our fantasies and urges dictate the course of our lives to a great extent, and when we wind up at the doors of despair, we say that we did it all for love.

The Voltec sorcery challenge is to treat sex in a new and non-ordinary way, thus liberating the static energy flow that sets in as a result of normal sexual activity. To treat sex in a non-ordinary way, we begin by thinking of it in terms of energy. Sexual thoughts and acts have great power, and tremendous energy is used when engaging in them. Therefore, in order to begin using this energy for new endeavors, we must save and store our sexual energy. We come to treat sex as a powerful act that can be used for much more than procreation. Sexual energy is the basic foundation for the building and harnessing of the energy body, or dreaming double. Without sufficient sexual energy, dreaming power is made extremely difficult.

I have personally found that long periods of sexual abstinence are excellent for the physical body, and that sexual expenditure dedicated to acts of dreaming are made much more potent because of such abstention. The propagation of our species is the number one evolutionary prerogative, so it makes sense that countermanding our reproductive instincts will allow us to pursue other, less human endeavors. Dedicate your sexual energy to a higher purpose. Create a special chamber, completely devoted to dreaming and sex magic. Set aside full moons for acts of sexual sorcery, and in this way you will begin tapping into that shadow of something that we all eventually take for granted. The fact is that, when sex becomes boring and routine for us, it fails to alter perception and this means that it fails to move the Assemblage Point.

Voltec sorcery begins with the non-ordinary handling of ordinary awareness. The specifics of Voltec sex magic will not be discussed here, as they are reserved specifically for the members of the Order of the Voltec, but I think that I have created quite a clear picture here of the various possibilities.

Dreaming was one of the major endeavors that led the ancient Toltecs into the unknown, and that is something that has not changed much over the many years since their reign. The average, ordinary individual treats dreams as nothing more that the strange disconnected thoughts that we have while we are asleep. Most people either have great difficulty remembering their dreams, or they cannot remember them at all. How the sorcerer treats and relates to dreams is a perfect example of a major not-doing. For us, dreams are real events. Granted, they are not events as we have come to know them throughout our lives, but they are genuine occurrences that take place at another level of awareness. Treating dreams in a way that is diametrically different than how we are socialized to treat them, leads us into the actuality of their true power and purpose. Dreaming takes on a new depth.

How do we begin? Well, first of all, we must treat dreaming as a non-ordinary sleeping situation. In the writing of

Carlos Castaneda, we discover the essentials of "setting up dreaming." The Voltec sorcerer is advised to have a special place set aside specifically for sorcery dreaming, because this automatically sets the Intent of non-ordinary dreaming into motion. Voltecs can build coffin like dreaming chambers, or fashion one out of a very small room in their dwelling. This place is intended for the practice of dreaming and must not be shared for any other purpose. The whole point of the maneuver is to focus and trap the second attention (non-ordinary awareness.) Our dreaming sorcery comes alive when it is given a purpose, just as do many of our hidden faculties. It takes extreme action and commitment in order to break into this unused flow of energy. This is one major area which differentiates most individuals who embrace a Toltec world view from the Voltec sorcerer. It is within our understanding and experience that it takes dramatic and sustained action in order to reach the Nightside. It takes even more action to immerse ourselves therein. This is where most magical schools of thought fail. They either stay at the level of philosophical and abstract musings, or they focus on pre-established rituals and routines to the point of stagnation.

    We actively seek to cultivate our own non-ordinary relationship with awareness and energy, and to this end we begin treating ordinary reality in non-ordinary ways. We transmute our sexual desires into the intent of the dreaming double, and we turn our sexual acts into powerful processes that give this intent the necessary energy to become self sustaining. The dreaming double feels this strange disturbance in one's normal energy flow, and acknowledges it by allowing us to experience our daily awareness in the depths of dreaming. The acquisition of power is achieved when the sorcerer finally experiences the reality of this kind of dreaming, as well as other non-ordinary perceptions that are a result of their efforts.

For the Voltec sorcerer, the most significant shifts of the Assemblage Point are self induced shifts caused by a willful and intentional change in their own frame of mind. An example of this would be to intentionally step back from a given situation and purposely try to view it from a different perspective. Once the perfect frame of mind is achieved, then appropriate behaviors can be implemented in order to stabilize the Assemblage Point on its new position. If you are having a difficult time in your career of choice and your attitude has deteriorated to the point of misery, try assuming a totally new perspective. Instead of talking about your woes to fellow coworkers during lunch, intentionally talk about their interests, or speak only of the productive things that are going on. Now, I realize that this sounds like a formula for a self help manual, but the fact is that through this active re-emphasis, the Assemblage Point will move and new, potent energies will be at you disposal. The first and most practical steps towards power are the achievement of a fluid state of being. Such mental and behavioral alterations, when performed intentionally will have a remarkable effect on you entire being. You will transcend what it means to be human and begin to comprehend the vastness of creation. Another pertinent side effect of this magical fluidity is that one learns how to slow down the aging process to a near grinding halt. This is because once we come to truly embody the knowledge that who we think we are is nothing more that a point of view, then we start to grasp the actual control that we have in our self definition. This, of course extends itself to the physical level, and thus we become capable of continually moving our assemblage points. Old age and death are the end result of the permanent fixation of the assemblage point on one given spot for too long. Youth and vitality are the byproduct of perceptual fluidity.

Nod and Beyond
Portal Ceremony: Gate of the Voltec
Wendigo V°

Introduction

A large part of the curriculum of the Voltec involves experiencing the perceptual spheres and paths on the Tree of Night. This "Tree" is, collectively, referred to as "Nod" (Nod 60: Nun 50, Vav 6 and Daleth 4 = 60). Nod, biblically speaking, is the region where Cain went after murdering Abel. This is also the land that Lilith established after leaving Adam. Nod, to the Voltec, is actual collective, specific locations of the Assemblage Point in which the Initiate can experience perceptual shifts among the Tree of Night. Since this is a fairly subjective experience, the Order of the Voltec has adopted using a Portal, through which a leap can be made. The energies of Nod are actual, concrete manifestations that exist on separate and often subtle planes of Awareness, but how each sorcerer interprets these potencies will often be influenced by the core subjective nature of the individual Voltec. Once the Initiate becomes comfortable with this procedure, s/he can make the same leap to that Position of the Assemblage Point anytime s/he wills to do so. The portal of the Voltec serves a multitude of sorcery functions. This portal will actually allow a Voltec sorcerer to establish contact with other Initiates during simultaneous workings despite any amount of physical distance between the participants. It can also be used in the process of the recapitulation to send energetic incarnations of one's past selves into the portal in order to help the sorcerer in their overall Voltec transformation away from the human form. This technique involves standing in front of the portal, looking at one's reflection and feeling ones past experiences being pulled in.

This specific portal ceremony has been used for years by the founding members of the Order of the Voltec with tremendous success, and what follows is the version we are presenting to all active members. It is, among many things, a way to continually and actively reach the dreaming body while fully awake. It is the Voltec preamble and key to heightened awareness, and as such it is one of our foundational workings. The Portal Ceremony will be done towards the beginning of all Voltec works of Greater Black Magic. The Ceremony is to be practiced alone by Diabolists (I°) before their personal work. This is to ensure that the Diabolist masters this practice before being called upon to use it in intense acts of Voltec sorcery. A beneficial side effect of this Portal Ceremony is the strengthening of (and working with) the "Double" which is very important, especially if the Initiate finds themselves leaning towards membership in the House of Yith within the Order of the Voltec.

Constructing the Portal

The Portal is constructed from a large piece of glass – the bigger the glass is the better. A piece that is as tall as the Initiate is ideal but a smaller one will work. Also, if one has the means, tapering the sides of the glass to form an elongated trapezoid is also desirable but not at all necessary. We leave much of the portal's physical appearance up to the creativity of the individual Voltec.

The glass should be cleaned during a state of meditation in which the Magician has focused his Intent and, if possible, has stopped his Internal Dialogue altogether.

Since the Portal represents access to the Subjective Universe and the unknown, it must be transformed into a black mirror. This is accomplished by coating one side of the glass with flat black spray paint. Multiple coats ensure a consistent and even covering. Again, this process is to be done while focusing your intent on creating a power object, capable of great feats of sorcery. This is the Initiates first object made specifically for Voltec sorcery and as such it should be made with care and kept for the duration of ones quest to Divinity.

Once this is done, devise a way for the glass to be stood or hung up so that when you stand in front of it, you can see your reflection. It is best to keep it towards the back wall of your ritual space. It's also important to keep it covered when not in use. I suggest building or buying an attractive frame for the portal and making special curtains to hang in front of it.

Portal Incense / Lighting

Incense is burned in front of the Portal so that the smoke rises between the participant(s) and the glass. The incense consists of 3 parts Wormwood and 1 part Sandalwood. Wormwood is an important herb within Voltec formulas. It was said to grow along the path of the serpent as he left Eden (the Dayside Tree). It is also known for its entheogenic properties, however using it as incense will not induce any altered states. Lighting may be adjusted according to the need of the sorcerer and the type of working. Sometimes it may be beneficial to place the lighting on either side of the portal in order to better reflect that which is without, and at other times it may be better to place the light sources behind the sorcerer, so that their reflection in the portal is that of a shadow figure.

The Portal Ceremony

This is a very simple, yet effective technique for shifting the Assemblage Point to a position in which different states of awareness can be engaged.

Light the Incense before the Portal and allow the smoke to rise between the glass and yourself. The room should only have enough light to barely make out your reflection in the glass. A single candle on the other side of the room is usually enough.

Clear your mind and, if you are able, stop the Internal Dialogue.

Fix your gaze upon the eyes of your shadowy reflection and know that you are seeing a completely different aspect of the Self.

Continue to gaze, while willing your awareness to shift places with your reflection.

Once you are confident that you are now looking out at the room from the inside of the portal, turn around and walk into Nod and conduct your working.

There may be some working specific elements added to this process on a working-to-working basis. (examples; gazing at a specific sigil instead of your reflection in order to gain access to specific Tunnels of Set, or the intoning of Mantras or power words, etc). These will be described as needed.

Internal Structure and Degree System of the Order of the Voltec

Departing from traditional religio-magical degree structures, the Order of the Voltec has approached the matter of initiation from a fresh perspective. The Tree of Night is the shadow, and therefore it has been conceived as being turned upside down. The initiation of the Voltec sorcerer is based completely on a foundation of Left Hand Path philosophy. This is why the degree structure of the Voltec is almost unrecognizable from a traditional perspective. The back magician does not strive to achieve a transcendental communion with the forces that they engage themselves with, but instead they seek to tap into, use and strengthen themselves with these powers. Most initiatory systems to date, start with the novice being placed in a probationary status in regard to the specific magical or religious order in question. This is the exploratory stage where the new initiate is exposed to the outer expressions of the organization, while the organization itself assesses and scrutinizes the beginner. The Voltec system is designed to challenge the initiate in uniquely personal ways, while retaining enough uniformity of practice so that every individual can benefit. For the new Voltec, action is the key to attainment. Once again, the ancient Toltecs regularly performed extraordinary feats of sorcery, and they did this by doing, not by speculating or projecting their hopes onto the objective universe. The adept of the Left Hand Path goes forward into a sea of the unknown, knowing that they will struggle to maintain their bearings in the dark Tunnels of Set. For the black adept, things are expected not to always make sense. The antinomian current dictates that once an energy pattern or set of beliefs becomes outmoded, then the resulting stasis must be rejected in favor of new areas of potentiality. The black adept has taken a vow to avoid stasis and to plunge head long into the land of Nod without the reassurance or comfort of the Known. The Voltec takes their accumulated power and knowledge and brings it into the shifting desert of shadows, where they transform the unknown emanations of the universe at large into perceivable, concrete realities.

Most initiatory systems, even those of the Left Hand Path persuasion, seem to be structured around levels of attainment that focus more on the subjective, individual experience of the initiate. A consensus in these systems revolves around ideas pertaining to interests of the organization in question, or the particulars of the magical system that the organization primarily relies upon. The initiates of the Voltec emphasize the linked consensual experiences of each sorcerer and how these experiences lead to agreed upon, actual results. What many initiatory systems lack in practicality, the Order of the Voltec has consistently striven to remedy.

The essence of our individuality as Left Hand Path practitioners is strongly connected to our ambition and drive as self-actualizing, creative beings. Each Voltec degree has, at its core, a set of practical attainments set out for the black magician to accomplish and master. This is in conjunction with units of fundamental Left Hand Path teachings and philosophies, as well as exploratory topics of varying complexity. Individuality is not only strongly encouraged, but watched for and carefully nurtured by each initiate's Voltec elder. The degrees of the Voltec are not places for the disenchanted student of the occult to hide from the world, but shadow power zones that allow the sorcerer to interact intimately and effectively with the daily world, while remaining essentially and energetically separate from it.

Initiatory Grade Structure of the Order of the Voltec

Diabolist I°

The first degree is that of the Diabolist, being representative of the conscious choice of the initiate to actively pursue the Left Hand Path. This a total rejection of Right Hand Path philosophy and dogma put into action. Initiates of the first degree will be required to articulate their understanding of the antinomian current, as well as their desire to commit to the Left Hand Path of attainment. The word Diabolist describes one who has made a commitment to the Prince of Darkness. This commitment from our perspective is the essence of antinomian existence and thought. The Diabolist will be challenged with putting Left Hand Path philosophy into daily practice in the every day world. Objective evidence of this is expected in the form of written updates, submitted on a regular basis to a II° mentor, who will be assigned to the new first degree upon being admitted into the Order. Included in the curriculum of the first degree will be a required reading list and the presentation of academic research pertaining to each module within the grade papers. No form of magical practice is required during this stage of Voltec initiation. Practicing black magicians may continue their regular sorcery pursuits, but the order does not mandate that they keep any type of formal documentation for order presentation. The first degree is a time of introspection dedicated to helping the Left Hand Path initiate internalize the concepts that they will eventually experience as they descend into the Tunnels. Unless the new initiate has been meritoriously advanced to the grade of Sorcerer because of prior achievement and natural ability, they can expect to remain in the first degree for at least one year. This estimated time limit is applicable due to the projected time for reading, writing and course work completion. The first degree initiate is not expected to affiliate with other members of this grade. They will not be admitted into an active Column until all the grade requirements have been met.

Sorcerer II°

The primary objective of the second degree initiate is to learn the fundamentals for saving, storing and redeploying personal energy. Without the redeployment of energy, any further progress on the path of the Voltec would be impossible. The sorcerer is expected to begin restructuring their lives in a way that is conducive to the saving of personal power. This includes such practices as actively losing self importance (becoming as shadow), erasing personal history and taking on new social roles that are dramatically different from those normally assumed. The second degree includes in its curriculum, the basic practices of Hatha Yoga. These practices are primarily limited to Asana (posture and sitting still for long periods of time) and breathing techniques. The yogas of concentration and visualization are reserved for those who have moved to the third degree. The Sorcerer is expected to have mastered, or be engaged in mastering certain chosen features of their daily world. This could include, but is not limited to undergraduate, graduate or doctoral levels of academic achievement, the fine arts, corporate and executive stature, athletic fitness and achievement, or any area of interest that the second degree finds they have a particular affinity with. The Sorcerer will be assigned up to three first degree protégées to guide, instruct and assess for second degree initiation.

The second degree Sorcerer will devote themselves to their own psychic and physical refinement before proceeding to the third degree. Major life problems such as severe financial mismanagement, morbid obesity or emotional/mental imbalance will disqualify the sorcerer from being accepted into either the House of Yith or the House of the Bloody Tongue. During the Sorcerer's time spent as a second degree, they will be watched and assessed by members of the IV°. This assessment is done to determine which of the two "Houses" of the Order will be most appropriate for the developing adept. Briefly, the House of the Bloody Tongue is aligned primarily with the arts of stalking, as described by Carlos Castaneda, and the House of Yith is concerned primarily with dreaming. These areas of exploration are the underlying current that guides each house, however, each grade within each house has its own agenda and special items of interest. Once the second degree Sorcerer has completed all of the necessary requirements of that degree, they will submit a letter to each of the order's houses. The letter will be a summary of their second degree work, and a rationalization for why they should be accepted into that particular house. The senior IV° of each house will then decide to which house the sorcerer belongs. Once the II° is notified of this, they will be ceremoniously accepted into their prospective House and the degree of either Bokhor III°, or that of P'hansigar III° will be conferred upon them.

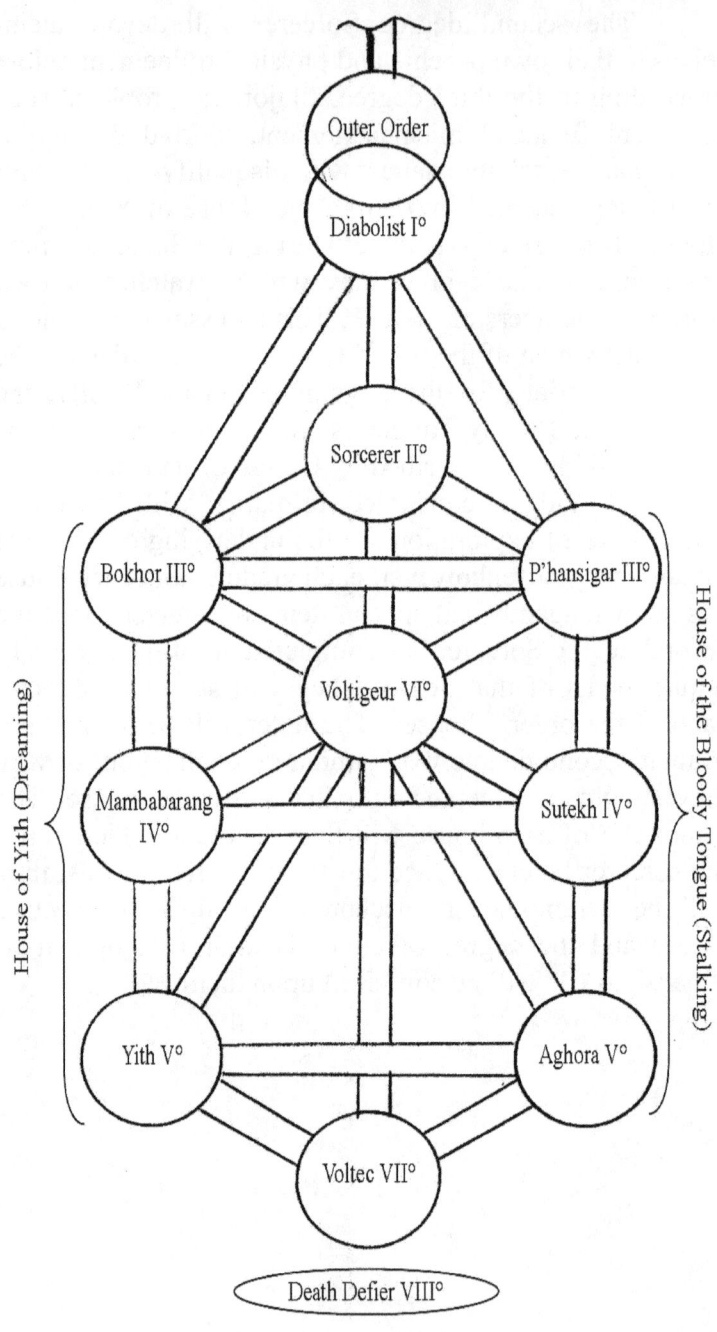

House of the Bloody Tongue

For those Voltec Initiates whom have natural inclinations towards the Stalker's Path, rather than the Dreamer's Path, the House of the Bloody Tongue offers an environment in which the Sorcerer can build upon his/her natural strengths and immediately apply the newly acquired skills of the Voltec to his/her personal development.

This split of approaches is temporary. The Voltec Initiate starts out on the Middle Pillar during their time as a I° and II° where they were not asked to even contemplate the differences between Dreaming and Stalking practices. This split is a necessary, progressive, step that usually can not be avoided. One is either a Stalker or a Dreamer. However, an important realization must be made. Just as individual starts on the Middle Pillar, they must also end up there as a VI° and VII° where, again, they will not acknowledge any difference between Stalking and Dreaming. Ultimately, the Voltec must master both for complete Perceptual Freedom. The Voltec Initiate will make this split knowing that during their time in either House, they will be also seeking ways to utilize their strengths to (Stalking for the House of the Bloody Tongue members) enhance their weaker abilities (Dreaming for the House of the Bloody Tongue members).

P'hansigar III°
"Blood Warrior"
Hod

During a Voltec's time as a Sorcerer II°, they were working in a very broad range of techniques in order to expand their Awareness. The P'hansigar continues this work while incorporating some new concepts. Within this degree, they will temporarily phase out most of the "ceremonial magic" practices and focus on some other forms of Shamanic Sorcery.

What is a Blood Warrior? The Voltec that has approached his/her Work within the Order of the Voltec will have one of two paths open for them. For those, within the House of the Bloody Tongue, a realization that they were not energetically aligned with the "Dreamers" approach (yet) and have to set their sights on reaching the same goals that dreamers seek, through acts of Stalking. For the P'hansigar, Assemblage Point shifts and movements are an arduous Battle. They have many obstacles to over come. All of their successes are predicated in the Victory that they must achieve over external and internal obstacles. Some Battles are small and others are a matter of life and death. The P'hansigar III°, will be accosted by all the unseen forces of all realms of existence. The House of the Bloody Tongue will help the OV Stalkers equip themselves with the knowledge and techniques to over come these obstacles.

How do we feel this is best accomplished, at this point? I have developed a system that I call "Bare Foot Sorcery". This system relies on a certain level of abandonment of Ceremonial Magical practices. The reduction of props and implements is also a feature to this minimal approach. This approach is also, very active. It requires one to move, to be decisive, and to directly act onto key points of a situation in order to affect its outcome. Bare Foot Sorcery (BFS) is an expansive system despite this minimalist approach. BFS allows the Initiate to shift/move his/her Assemblage Point without the use of ceremonial props or extensive preparations. To act on a moments notice, decisively and without hesitation is a skill that will be developed slowly as the P'hansigar improves their abilities within the OV. BFS also requires the P'hansigar to work towards removing the human drive for comfort. The P'hansigar is not concerned with the human drive for constant comfort and avoidance of pain. Discomfort, if encountered legitimately through the course of one's progress, should be expected as a temporary price to be paid for non-human advancement.

BFS, is complete Immersion into an environment or select portions of an environment in order to accomplish specific tasks. Rather than working within a "ritual chamber" you will work your sorcery outdoors, in the wilderness, in the city streets, in towns and in the mountains. Wherever you may be, you will be equipped to access personal energy and re-deploy it for any reason you see fit.

Other than Bare Foot Sorcery the P'hansigar will work with these other concepts:

Assemblage Point "Snapping"

The P'hansigar will be instructed on methods of a new concept called Assemblage Point Snapping. This concept removes the "cloudiness" experienced by Initiates as they shift the Assemblage Point. The AP often must pass through various positions in order to arrive at its destination, which often obscures the experiences of that Position. AP Snapping allows the practitioner to shift the AP, seemingly, instantly to the new location, thereby providing an undistorted perception.

Polishing the Tonal

The P'hansigar will become fluid in all consensual reality situations. This means while augmenting a situation with BFS, the Initiate will utilize concepts of verbal manipulation, body language, charm, social blending, proxemics, etc. The Will can eventually be sharpened so that conscious effort for such manipulation of social laws will become obsolete. Polishing the Tonal will lead one to that end.

Filter Mastery and Filter Removal

Within the II°, the Voltec Sorcerer was made Aware of Perceptual Filters and how the shape our experiences. With this newly sharpened Awareness the P'hansigar can intentionally employ these filters to Perceive a specific element within various Positions of the Assemblage Point thereby making it possible focus on only the immediately applicable portions of the experience. The P'hansigar will also learn to master the removal of all Perceptual Filters. This is made possible through the practice of Emotional Control, Sobriety, Abandon, further mastery of the Voltec Portal, Dreaming (yes, even though we are Stalkers in the House of the Bloody Tongue we still must utilize Dreaming), Inaccessibility and other forms of Control.

Downward Path Sorcery

As described in my book, *"Downward Path into Nod",* the Initiate is lead through a progression of Shadow Self manipulations in which both temporary and permanent changes are made. The Initiate is lead step by step through each "Power Zone" upon the Voltec Tree of Night in order to accumulate the effects governed by each Position of the Assemblage Point therein. A major concern is the reduction of the influence of the Dayside Self while operation within the Awareness of the Shadow Self.

Forked Tongue Sorcery

The P'hansigar is expected to work on the unification of the two spheres of magic. It is obvious that Left Hand Path magic is used daily on our quest for Perceptual Freedom, however Right Hand Path systems must also be used toward LHP goals. The Initiate need not document the hows and whys of their pursuit of Forked Tongue Sorcery, however they will be expected to work within ANY system towards the goals associated with the Voltec Current.

Martial Sorcery

The P'hansigar's true accomplishment is the ability to act. There is little "meditation" involved. The P'hansigar sees opportunity, he/she can sense an opening and knows where to deploy his/her energies. If the P'hansigar is physically able to do so, they are urged to study a martial art under a qualified instructor. The student should make every effort to learn the physical aspects in a manner that is both beneficial to his/her health and in a functional manner capable of deployment for self defense. As well as health/self defense the student should take it upon themselves to learn the history of that particular art and any energetic/magical/spiritual elements that they can find. A residual effect of Martial Arts that will be of service to the Blood Warrior is decisiveness. The Initiate must be able to act without hesitation in the safest possible way. In the House of the Bloody Tongue, one must learn the importance of changing themselves in order to change all life's situations. These changes often do not come with a time allowance and must be enacted immediately. The practice of Martial Arts is also a very good way of silencing the internal dialogue in an active way. Instead of Stopping the World by gazing or quiet meditation, the Initiate can do these things with Active Energy. With these things in mind, it becomes almost impossible to separate these Martial Sorcery concepts from Bare Foot Sorcery. Included in these sphere of study is Weaponcraft which will be elaborated upon in later documents.

Environmental Sorcery

This aspect of BFS enables the Initiate to Draw Energy from natural organic medium. The traditional elements of fire, earth, air and water will be mastered along with other natural phenomenon such as weather occurrences (snow, rain, fog, tornados, darkness, etc) and use of terrain (streams, mountains, desert, sewers, basements, forests, etc). Control of survival situations and over Initiatory pursuits in these environments will lead the P'hansigar to an increased ability to sense his/her impact upon the organic world and provide a renewed sense of their actual place within the Universe.

Life Extension

Through physical fitness, diet and energetic awareness the P'hansigar is expected to make an effort to increase the quality of his/her health and to buy more time to accomplish the difficult tasks set forth within the Voltec Current. In society we have become tolerant of others shortcomings and as a result of this tolerance, we have made things easier on ourselves. The will power to eat less and eat healthier should NOT be a huge strain on a Voltec Sorcerer. Exercise should not be viewed as something unassociated with Sorcery. But this is the way many people think. Today is the day to start. This is not a self help, "you can do it" speech…it is an appeal to your higher self to establish the physical representation of it to conquer all modes of existence.

These are just a few concepts or "spheres of interest" for the P'hansigar III° and many more will be addressed as one moves along in the Voltec Current. These concepts will be explained in greater detail to those whom are involved within the House of the Bloody Tongue.

Beyond the III° in the Order of the Voltec is very specialized and reserved for those individuals whom have gone beyond the average Initiate and has successfully applied all the principles described within the first 3 degrees. I will only briefly touch upon each of the last two degrees within the House of the Bloody Tongue because such information regarding these degrees is tailored for the individual in question.

Sutekh IV°
"Crosser of the Desert"
Geburah

The fourth degree, within both Houses, is a tremendous step. The Voltec goes from merely being influenced by the Voltec Current to Immersing completely into it. The Sutekh IV° is the "Crosser of the Desert" meaning that they have acquired the abilities to traverse the Desert of Awareness. They are Nomads of Perception in that they refuse to settle within one mode of operation and utilize any technique that they encounter.

Unlike the P'hansigar, the Sutekh IV° will invest time in acedemic learning, occult research and theoretical pursuits. They will also begin to study the Ceremonial Magick of the Order of the Voltec (as described with the book *Twilight Undone*). Influenced by Night and Life through Death, Beginning the Process of Isolating the Self from the Human Condition. The Sutekh moves the Assemblage Point through techniques of chaos magic and tradition western high magickal techniques. Mastery of Ceremonial Vampyrism and Shape Shifting is pursued as well as ceasing all personal and energy consuming habits and patterns.

The Initiate will receive information on the various forms of inorganic life and instructions on dealing with them. Unlike the P'hansigar, who strives to conduct all of his/her operations with little to no tools or preparations, the Sutekh IV° will construct Voltec specific ritual implements and learn a complete system of ritual magic that includes energy manipulation exercises, invocations, evocations, imprinting personal experiences upon the Voltec Current, reading impressions within the Voltec Current, etc.

Aghora V°
"Voltec Monk"
Binah

This degree is obviously the most bizarre of all of the House of the Bloody Tongue degrees (by Human standards). Within the V° the Voltec Initiate is instructed on the Sexual Sorcery of the Voltec (described at length in the book "Chalice and the Serpent") and on the techniques of Laboratory Sorcery in which the Voltec shifts their Assemblage Point by performing scientific processes that are aimed at producing a product to be used in Sorcery.

The Aghora V° is a degree of renounced perceptions of society and of the Human Condition. The V° has

has disassembled the Human Mold and has Erased Personal History. They will speak very little of themselves and what they do. They will reduce social endeavors except where completely necessary to maintain a some what functional consensual life.

Acknowledging the Unknowable and things beyond Human Condition by experiencing states of "no-mind". Atavistic Resurgence and other non-human techniques are utilized in preparation of an Initiates move to the degree of Voltigeur. Influenced by the Endless Night of Space and Immortality. All practices are unique to each Voltec Monk and should be as alien as possible.

It is within this degree that the Initiate considers the possibility of Death Defiance and begins to restructure the their entire energy field and inventory to prepare for the VI° and beyond.

This concludes my overview of the degrees of the House of the Bloody Tongue for public review. Again, we have included as much as possible about each degree, however, a detailed description of the III°+ is unnecessary for individuals outside of the organizations for the information regarding them would be full of terms that the reader would not be familiar with nor be interested in.

Wendigo V°
Voice of the Downward Path

House of Yith

The House of Yith, as mentioned earlier, is for Voltec Initiates whom have satisfied the requirements of the I° and II° and believe themselves to be "Dreamers".

Bokhor III°
"Those Who Work with Both Hands"
Netzach

The third degree of the House of Yith holds the title of Bokhor. The sorcerer who has been given this title is now positioned at the entrance to the halls of dreaming. The Bokhor is concerned with discovering the reality of their double nature. All III°s should have read the complete works of Castaneda. Beginning dreaming exercises will include keeping a dream record to enhance dream recall, finding and utilizing dreaming objects and dream shape shifting. The degree of Bokhor is also dedicated to exploring and developing the sorcerer's relationship with inorganic beings (i.e. Loa, Orisha, deities, etc.) through the use of ritual and magic. The yoga of the Bokhor is that of the path of devotion. This is Bhakti yoga, which concerns itself with the adherent's devotion to particular deities.

The Bokhor is a specialist who has already matured in the arts of sorcery. They know what kinds of magic works best for them, and they perform this magic with real, concrete results. Through the practice of lesser and greater black magic, the third degree becomes intimately acquainted with a concept that the Toltecs referred to as Intent. They spend their time during this degree refining magical practices, conducting research for themselves and the Order. The Bokhor works with both hands, meaning that they have transcended the need to define their work in terms that have either a positive or negative value. The Bokhor will study and document the living connection between their magical practices and their dreaming experiences and practices. Sigil magic, the creation of servitors, magical invocation, spirit possession, shamanic divination systems, witchcraft (brujeria) and ceremonial magic are a few of the specialties of the Bokhor. The major task of the third degree is to begin molding their everyday world into a work of art that is a result of their own power. The Bokhor unites the energies of opposites, and with this comes the understanding that the magic they perform is the Not-Doing of the every day world. The Bokhor's not-doings are the elements of the basic foundation for their future success in dreaming.

Those initiates of the third degree, who are so inclined, may decide to form a Column of the Order of the Voltec. The Column structure is very akin to the Grotto of the CoS, or the Pylon of the ToS. It is a group of black magicians who have come together in order to exchange ideas, practice group ritual workings and to generally add their multiplied energy to the goals of the Column, or individual. A Column may consist of no more than fifteen members. It has been our experience that any more than this tends to dilute the Intent of the group and create unnecessary social complexities. If a Column is in danger of becoming too big, then another third degree Bokhor may be enlisted to form a second Column based out of the first one. A Column may only be formed with the permission of the Council of Set, and the application for such a group must include the fundamental purpose(s) of the proposed Column. Columns of the Order of the Voltec must consist of at least one third degree, but may include as many third or second degree members as naturally occurs, up until the maximum number is reached. Fourth degree members may not formally belong to a Column, but they can serve as guest speakers, facilitators or instructors upon the request of the Column Head. A Column is expected to contribute regularly to the Order as a whole. These contributions may take any form. They may be special group workings, presented as a demonstration, or works of research, art or literature, compiled by the Column Head. A Column is not limited in its creative purposes, however in order to exist, it must have a recognizable level of activity.

Before acceptance and initiation into the sect of the Mambabarang IV°, the Bokhor will have to present a capstone project, consisting of one original magical/shamanistic technique, practice or concept that has been thoroughly conceived of and utilized by themselves and at least one other third degree. Successful completion and presentation of the capstone project (which will be reviewed by the Council of Set) will qualify the Bokhor to become eligible to pursue the basic requirements for admittance to the IV°. This requirement of a "Capstone" project also exists as part of the House of the Bloody Tongue advancement requirements.

Degrees VI through VIII are not presented to the public at this time. Specific questions dealing with the details of these degrees can be directed to the Council of Set.

Mambabarang IV°
"The Double"
Chesed

When the third degree, Bokhor, has completed all assigned course work and tasks, they will be asked to present a written treatise explaining their understanding of dreaming as a concrete realm of action and possibility. This work must also include a detailed synopsis of the third degree's experience and achievements on the Left Hand Path and within the order. The Sect of the Mambabarang concerns itself with mastering practices of concentration, visualization and basic dreaming skills. It is expected that the individual Mambabarang will be able to remain capable of second gate dreaming practices. Dreaming experiences are to be kept in a special journal, which can be used for the basis of any academic presentation or to simply track the Mambabarang's progress over the years. The Voltec initiate who has reached the Sect of the Mambabarang has begun to embody, in their very essence, the non-human qualities of the Unknown. Mambabarangs have successfully learned how to focus their Will on whatever they desire, and thus manipulate the power of Intent in that direction.

The Voltec initiate at this stage is given various administrative duties in order to aid the Council of Set in its many functions. The Mambabarang will be assigned at least one second degree member to continually assess for the possibility of further advancement. The Mambabarang will also be the active point of contact for those of the third degree when the needs of the third degree and below have to be addressed.

Just as the IV° Sutekh of the Bloody Tongue are devoted to the great god Set, so too are the Mambabarang devoted to the feminine face of eternal darkness. If the Order of the Voltec were to have a priesthood, the fourth degree would most resemble it. The fourth degree practices concern ritual techniques for dreaming and moving the Assemblage Point, gathering energy vampyrically, working with sorcery movements to strengthen dreaming and the yoga of thought. A Voltec variation of Raja yoga will be practiced and used to refines the fourth degree's ability to visualize and sustain dreaming images.

The Bhakti Yoga of the Bokhor is taken to the extreme in the Sect of the Mambabarang, and the union of dark divinity with the individual Voltec sorcerer is the desired result. Ritual sorcery invocation is used to forcefully move the Assemblage Point away from its customary position, with the result of acquiring the powers of deity. The Mambabarang will be called on to refine all practices within the Order, and to develop their own sorcery movements which must facilitate either dreaming, the movement of the Assemblage Point or the mastery of Intent. After the Mambabarang has thoroughly demonstrated and documented their ability at second gate dreaming practices, they will be eligible for application to the grade of Yith. As a prerequisite, the Mambabarang will be asked to present all of their IV° work in the form of a personal account, documenting their progress through the IV° tasks. At this point, the Voltec initiate may decide to remain at the IV° level indefinitely, for the demands of the V° and higher may not be suitable or compatible with the every day existence of the Voltec Sorcerer.

Yith V°
"Those Who Have Risen"
Chokmah

The fourth degree in the House of Yith is conferred upon those Voltecs who have displayed consistent talent in the art of dreaming, as well as a primary, internal desire to completely transcend all that is human. By human, I mean those energetic conditions that create obvious limitations of the Self. The fourth degree requires mastery over the flow and concept of time itself, and those who have reached this Realm of Shadow will see the results of their sorcery in all aspects of their not so mundane lives. No further details for the degree of Yith can, or will be made public.

The Council of Set and the Three Voices of the Current

The organization that is the Order of the Voltec is directed by its founders. However, there is a system in place that will allow others to assume control after the founders have moved on.

The Council of Set is responsible for the smooth operation and handling of the group. They oversee projects and resolve any potential disputes. The Council of Set has three "chairs", one for each "Voice" of the Voltec Current.

The position and responsibilities of each of the three Voices is as follows:

Voice of the Backwards Way: This is the head of the Order of the Voltec and represents the Middle Pillar of the Voltec Tree of Night. This Voice must be spoken by an individual that holds a VI° or higher.

Voice of the Downward Path: This is the representative of the House of the Bloody Tongue. This Voice can must be spoken by an individual that holds a IV° or higher.

Voice of the Outer Darkness: This Voice is the head of the House of Yith. This voice must be spoken by an individual that holds a IV° or higher.

The Voices of the Current are not presented as authority figures to be "followed". These individuals have, simply, made themselves accessible to the Voltec Current and their availability is designed to translate the impressions of the Voltec Current and to record the dealings of the Order of the Voltec within the Current for future Cycles.

Affiliation and Admissions Policies of the Order of the Voltec

So if this text has made sense, and you think you would like to know a little more or are considering Active Membership, there are a few things you can do and a few things you should know.

We encourage interested individuals to visit our website at http://www.redpath.imagitronix.co.za/voltec

In order to become involved with the Order of the Voltec an individual needs to have regular access to a computer with internet access. We conduct out projects within our "Yahoo!" groups. All applicants must be, at least, 18 years of age.

The Outer Order is setup to allow potential members an opportunity to access the group. It is a Yahoo group and can be found at: http://groups.yahoo.com/group/order_of_the_voltec/ This Yahoo group contains a sampling of our writings, publication announcements, discussions relevant to the Order of the Voltec. It is an excellent way to get in touch with the directors of the group and its other members. It's open to anyone who requests entry, however we expect each new member of the Outer Order to write and post a little self-introduction to the group. Be aware that there is a 90 day expiration of Outer Order membership. We feel that is long enough for a person to make an informed decision about Active Membership. If an individual remains silent and makes no attempt at contribution or contact, they will be removed after 90 days.

Membership in the Order of the Voltec is not like other "occult" or "magickal" organizations. We expect participation in our projects and contributions to discussions and in written form. Financial contributions are only voluntary but appreciated.

If you make the decision to apply for active membership, just fill out the form in the "Files" directory in the Yahoo group and email it to the contacts provided.

The point of importance is the willingness to actually do the work. Many people want to take part in the online discussions or to be told what to do, however the Order of the Voltec is looking for competent magicians whom are self motivated. The reward of your efforts will make themselves obvious and the directors of the OV will notice.

In my book *"The Downward Path into Nod"*, Iremoch VI° provides a short commentary of the Order of the Voltec...

"A Voltec Sorcerer is a breaker of boundaries; a black magician who has reached an energetic and developmental threshold. We are the holders of an ancient configuration, keepers of a monumental edifice erected thousands of years past by masters of the force of Intent. They are still there, some of them, buried deep beneath the deserts of the American South West and Mexico. They continue to dream and they still are Aware. That very same force that drove these men and women of antiquity to break the boundaries of the Human Condition has coursed through the centuries, being shaped anew by those who have had the potential to express its abstract commands best. The core teachings of our Sorcery have always been the same, but with each new cycle came new realizations. What we Westerners have come to call the Left Hand Path, has

been redefined and invigorated by our experiences and Silent Knowledge. The Order of the Voltec creates, within its many faceted chambers, a place and perceptual context for black magicians of the highest caliber. The traditional and primary goals of the Left Hand Path have been distilled through our own brand of Shadow Alchemy and we have worked hard for years to draw upon and purify only the most essential ideas and techniques from shamanic practices around the world, particularly that of the Toltecs. At our very core, we still retain that definitive expectation of what the Left Hand Path really is. It is the never ending quest of the Sorcerer to free themselves of human limitations, fortifying themselves against the universal tides of entropy and thus achieving a state of existence which in no way resembles that of the ordinary modern human. The strengthening of our consciousness and the retention of the individuality, past the point of physical death, are inevitable results of our combined efforts. Fear is a Voltec Sorcerer's Ally and Death walks next to each one of our kind. We are born onto the Nightside, and thus begin our apprenticeship. We knowingly leave the comforts of the world and look into the night; the face of the Unknown. For the Voltec Sorcerer, Power is earned through action and our words weave the reality of the world around us. If you belong here you will know. So will we."

Conclusion?

Each individual exists alone on a completely energetic level. The Right Hand Path view tends to see human beings as minute extensions of an omnipotent god-force, which in their ideology represents a higher perfected humanity. When the average woman or man comes to the end of their lives, they "pass on" and are subsequently re-absorbed into this greater being. The deity experiences multiplicity through its extensions because being an undifferentiated singularity, it cannot know duality directly. This cosmic relation gives rise to what is commonly referred to by mystics as "mara" or the illusion of reality and the individual self. I believe that what may have happened here is that the mystical and Right Hand Path traditions have confused the ego and base personality with the concept of individuality. Thousands of years of conditional morality, power seeking and misunderstood spiritual revelations have clouded the issue even more. According to the Toltec tradition, of which Voltec sorcery is a development, when the average person dies they are indeed re-absorbed into a field of awareness which has bestowed individual awareness upon them at the moment of biological conception. Unlike the adherents of the Right Hand Path, the Voltec sorcerer strives to fortify their individuality in whatever ways possible, and to defy death is the ultimate goal and achievement. This is not only possible, but also has become an evolutionary prerogative for those of us who reach to these depths. Wherever you may find yourself on the Nightside of the Left Hand Path, rely on your feelings and accumulated personal power and keep the ultimate goal always in sight.

Bibliography

Castaneda, Carlos. *The Teachings of Don Juan: A Yaqui Way of Knowledge*. New York: Simon and Schuster, 1968.

Castaneda, Carlos. *Tales of Power*. New York: Simon and Schuster, 1974

Castaneda, Carlos. *A Separate Reality: Further Conversations with Don Juan*. New York: Simon and Schuster, 1971.

Castaneda, Carlos. *The Second Ring of Power*. New York: Simon and Schuster, 1977.

Castaneda, Carlos. *The Power of Silence: Further Lessons of Don Juan*. New York: Simon and Schuster, 1987.

Castaneda, Carlos. *Journey to Ixtlan: The Lessons of Don Juan*. New York: Simon and Schuster, 1972.

Castaneda, Carlos. *The Fire From Within*. New York: Simon and Schuster, 1984.

Castaneda, Carlos. *The Eagle's Gift*. New York: Simon and Schuster, 1981.

Castaneda, Carlos. *The Art of Dreaming*. New York: HarperCollins, 1993.

Feather, Ken Eagle. *A Toltec Path: a user's guide to the teachings of Don Juan Matus, Carlos Castaneda, and other Toltec Seers*. Norfolk, VA: Hampton Roads, 1992.

LaVey, Anton. *The Satanic Bible*. New York: Avon Books, 1969.

Carroll, Peter J. *Liber Null & Psychonaut: an Introduction to Chaos Magic*. San Francisco: Red Wheel/Weiser, LLC, 1987.

Grant, Kenneth. *The Nightside of Eden*. London, England Skoob Books Publishing 1994

Wendigo V° *Downward Path into Nod*. Trenton N.J. Voltec Publishing 2007

Wendigo V° *Energetic Sorcery on the Voltec Tree of Night*. Trenton N.J. Voltec Publishing 2008.

Iremoch VI° *Sorcery of Perception*. Trenton N.J. Voltec Publishing 2008

The Nine Not-Doings of the Voltec

1) We seek to become as no-thing, knowing that only in formlessness can true perceptual freedom be experienced.

2) We denounce the concept of ego preservation and "isolate intelligence", knowing that to seek this in any way would hinder us from the infinite perceptual possibilities that awareness is.

3) We denounce the trappings of conventional society, in so far as these trappings are set to calcify our attention. Only when a conventional outlook or idea becomes Not-Doing for us individually do we seek to embody it. This is true antinomianism.

4) We denounce the use of Black Magic, or the manipulation of the life force for obtaining power over other individuals for common place ends. This does not include the use of heightened awareness for defensive or measures of self-preservation.

5) We refuse to ever speak openly about the O.V. with non-O.V. members, and questions concerning ones membership are to be appropriately deflected. Any affiliate of an Order member who expresses intense interest in the O.V. should be directed to the Order web page or encouraged to e-mail a third or fourth ring member.

6) We seek to destroy anything that may augment our self importance. This does not include those energetic differences that make us what we are.

7) We seek to de-structure ourselves in a harmonious way, rejecting those aberrant practices and behaviors that do not lend themselves to control and sobriety. The teachings of the Voltec are never to be used as justification for self-indulgence.

8) As members of the Order of the Voltec, we must demonstrate competence and mastery over our dayside awareness. We must seek to impeccably engage ourselves with the world of human affairs, not withdrawing from it or denouncing it.

9) We are prepared upon entering the O.V. to acknowledge our own eventual death as a change in energetic form and existence, maintaining that we have continually worked to fortify our individual awareness and thus aspire to true immortality.

www.ingramcontent.com/pod-product-compliance
Lightning Source LLC
Chambersburg PA
CBHW031636160426
43196CB00006B/439